DEPARTMENT OF

Speculative Facts

TABLE OF CONTENTS

Lietje Bauwens and Quenton Miller

An Introduction to Speculative Facts

"A fact, at its base, is a kind of social contract." Or so concluded one contemporary expert on facts—professional fact-checker Alex Carp. Reviewing factual claims by journalists on a daily basis for the *New York Times Magazine*, he saw cracks in the once-held belief in facts, as an objective, rock-solid ground on which our political, scientific and social reality can be built. To tease out this alleged social nature of facts, we asked Carp and his colleague Jamie Fisher to discuss their profession, which took place via an e-mail exchange. Weren't fact-checkers supposed to be the rational answer to irrational times? What can we learn about the politics of facts when such apparent guardians of truth flirt with post-truth ideas?

We observed that many artists and writers working with similar questions about the social nature of facts tend to a more speculative approach. By including contingency and the unknown, it becomes possible to construct alternative futures that are more emancipated than our current present. Yet as much as speculation is necessary for producing new political strategies and imaginaries, beyond Western-centrism and knowledge that suits the powerful, it also has the potential to erode even more trust in institutions, governments, and perhaps social life itself.

The Department started out of the neologism "Speculative Facts" to express our concern about this friction between two separate terms that seem both loaded and at times contradictory. Inspired by the other SF, or Science Fiction, we decided to think speculation through facts, and facts through speculation, by bringing them together in one concept. Firstly, we invited four (performance) artists to re-write, re-perform, and re-design the e-mail exchange between the two fact-checkers. Triggered by the questions raised by their interventions, we continued by inviting writers, philosophers and artists to speculate on facts, to fact-check speculations, and look at forms of agreement or facticity, with the idea of finding new types of social contracts with which we can anchor ourselves.

As a ground to work from, we proposed the following working definition of what a speculative fact could be:

> **Speculative fact** | **1** A contract about proof with stakes in the futures it enables and the experiences it comes from. | **2** A non-anthropocentric fact, allowing for complex stories and collective types of causalities. | **3** The tension field between building trust, and stretching or questioning what is proved or taken to be true.

Facts

Before the notion of facts solidified into its modern meaning, the concept was shaped by many disciplines, functions, contingencies and inextricably linked to narrative practices and aesthetics. Up to the end of the 1700s the German word *Tatsache*, meaning "matter of fact," was still used to describe biblical miracles that might or might not have taken place. In their modern context, facts first emerged in law, which used many theatrical and narrative devices. The participatory ways of legal fact-finding by law jurors have played a significant role in the cultural division of the concept. This "unit of proof" was picked up from law by historians who started to focus more on document-oriented history and to prefer first-hand witnesses over citations to authority. Via travel reporting and historiography, in which things seen and experienced were described, facts also made their way into the news and, in the process, transformed from a category limited to human actions and deeds into one that included also non-human phenomena. It was only in the early seventeenth century that lawyer, historian and natural philosopher Francis Bacon brought the term

1
Barbara J. Shapiro, *A Culture of Fact: England, 1550–1720* (Ithaka, NY: Cornell University Press, 2003).

2
Alex Carp, "History for a Post-Fact America," *The New York Review of Books* (19 October, 2018), https://www.nybooks.com/daily/2018/10/19/history-for-a-post-fact-america/

3
The phrase "alternative facts" was introduced by Kellyanne Conway in 2017 and then cultivated by Donald Trump as Fox News changed their slogan to "most watched, most trusted," seemingly suggesting that truth is determined by ratings.

4
Alex Carp, *History for a Post-Fact America*.

"fact" to the British scientific community where its meaning changed into a "theory-free" representation of empirical reality.[1]

Journalism provides many examples of how fact-construction is part of culture, one where aesthetics have always played a role. Early modern journalism blurred what we now call facts with love intrigues, fictions and satires. In the seventeenth century news could be sung or rhymed, and factual information was often transmitted through fiction. History and current events could be recounted by imaginary characters, famously in the eighteenth century by Mr. Spectator in London, who discussed news with other fictional archetypes like Sir Andrew Freeport and Captain Sentry. "Understanding the world through stories is as old as human civilization" Alex Carp wrote, "but building those stories from evidence, and building that evidence from facts, is a relatively recent development."[2]

Today we see again how the meaning of facts is being changed and questioned through the introduction of "alternative facts."[3] When "trolls" are faking online news and Baltic hacker communities, referring to themselves as "elves," have to gather to safeguard the truth, it feels like our present facts are in the hands of fairytale figures. Between 2014 and 2018, more than two fact-checking organizations were founded each month. Are they a way of working out a broader anxiety about the nature of our political, cultural, economic, social and ethical debates—we have too many facts, and still not enough—or a subconscious recognition that facts themselves have lost some of their power?[4] In his text on facts and trust in Forensic Architecture, which operates both in the artistic and legal arena, journalist Robert Trafford writes: "new rules of mass communication, born of new technological possibilities, have created a new political playing field, and in the process have laid bare the *constructedness* of facts, in ways that our existing social-political consensus has proved entirely unable to respond to."

Philosopher Bruno Latour has been a prominent actor in the cultural meaning of facts, emphasizing their social construction. He shifted to studying the politics and sociology behind, and thus within, facts instead of facts themselves. How, where and by whom are facts created and accepted? Latour's theory is an important break with the idea that scientific facts are inevitable and "theory-free," which is one of many ways that the word had been defined throughout history.[5] At the same time, it is a risky and controversial flirt with post-modern and relativist ideas in which facts are completely undermined because everything is true from another perspective. Latour has responded to this critique by saying that he never intended to move *away* from facts, but only move *closer* to facts; not to fight empiricism but to renew it[6] by enlarging the concept of experience in order to escape from a purely anthropological definition. Every experience is saturated with interpretations and ideas, and relies on a network of human and non-human actors. Latour proposes a realism that doesn't focus on "matters of fact" but on "matters of concern"—how to make stories matter to such an extent that the topic at hand becomes an *issue* and triggers debate? What world are you helping to make possible through the ways in which you formulate and problematize facts? Does the fact that facts are constructed, never isolated and always political, mean that they cannot also be true?

5
S.J. Ten Hagen, "How 'Facts' Shaped Modern Disciplines: The Fluid Concept of Fact and the Common Origins of German Physics and Historiography," *Historical Studies in the Natural Sciences*, Vol. 49, no. 3 (2019): 300–37.

6
Bruno Latour, "Why Has Critique Run out of Steam? From Matters of Fact to Matters of Concern," *Critical Inquiry 30,* (2004): 225–48.

7
Alex Kofman, "Bruno Latour, The Post-Truth Philosopher, Mounts a Defense of Science," *The New York Times Magazine* (25 October, 2018), https://www.nytimes.com/2018/10/25/magazine/bruno-latour-post-truth-philosopher-science.html

Truth.
It's more important now than ever.

Around the time the *New York Times Magazine* wrote an extensive article about Latour, whom in their headline they call "the post-truth philosopher"[7], the newspaper changed their slogan to "Truth. It's more important now than ever." It was at that moment that the Department of Speculative Facts invited the two fact-checkers from that same newspaper to start their shared e-mail reflection. The fact-checkers were very protective of the magazine's policies on fact(checking). Therefore, their exchange became more of a personal portrait of their daily experiences and the way their jobs had changed, than an insight into the politics of fact-checking procedures. "As we both know from working on a certain philosopher's profile, there's something philosophical in the procedural elements of breaking the sentence down, a limited kind of philosophy that makes axioms but doesn't necessarily proceed to assemble greater truths," they write in one of their early emails. As Latour's name was never mentioned or confirmed by the two fact-checkers, this association remains entirely speculative.

Speculation

Latour is linked to a large range of new, or renewed, interests in speculative philosophical theories, within both academia and the art world, which acknowledge a world beyond a human-centered cognitive scope. These contemporary speculative philosophies claim that we already live in a speculative world, constructed through uncontrollable (financial and algorithmic) fictions and propositions. Enlightened, human-centered and post-modern forms of critique, in which critique becomes an end in itself, are insufficient to deal with this contingent world. Instead of inward and stagnating critical judgments, speculative philosophies put their focus on reinvesting in new grand narratives in which the human (experience) is not centered, and fictions are not the opposite of reality but the source of its creation. Tristan Garcia is one of those object-oriented philosophers who not only theorizes *about* non-human subjectivities, but who also negotiates the boundaries of his own human subjectivity by writing from the perspective of, for example, a chimpanzee, Jesus, or a robot. In the interview included in this publication, he discusses his position as a writer, from which he attempts to go beyond himself, while always failing to become something truly "other": "Writing literature confronts me with the limits of my own language and form of life, the way I perceive and experience the world."

Along similar lines, speculative realism argues that it is only possible to deal with this already speculative reality by developing a speculative approach to it—one that is nonetheless rooted in our cognitive capacities. Speculative realism is a rational project: by accepting that which exists outside of human perception as "real," it becomes possible to inject the imaginary within our knowledge apparatus. In order to deal seriously with, for example, issues of privacy and data, we should learn to think in the contingent terms of algorithms; and a solution for the climate crisis should be as abstract, pluri-local, multi-systemic and trans-generational as the problem it wishes to address. Speculative discursive practices are not only able to map out the space of reason, but also negotiate its boundaries, pushing beyond its limits in the search for new ground.

Artist and curator Sepake Angiama attempts to collapse the linearity of space and time through collectively written science-fiction scenarios, some of which are included in this publication. She is inspired by writer Alexis Pauline Gumbs, who, in her story *Evidence*, receives letters from her future self living in a post-capitalist society. By taking newspaper headlines as a starting point, she uses journalistic facts to subsequently speculate upon their meaning, consequences and origins: facts not as the end but only the beginning. Hyperstitions, a trendy concept amongst speculative thinkers, are exactly this: fictions that cause the conditions that subsequently make them become real, coming *from* the future and retroactively changing both our present and past.

8
Lietje Bauwens, "Nieuwe ecologieen voor de zintuigen, in gesprek met Didier Debaise," *nY42*, June 25, 2020, https://www.ny-web.be/artikels/introductie-ny42/

9
Isabelle Doucet, "Narrate, Speculate, Fabulate: Didier Debaise and Benedikte Zitouni in Conversation with Isabelle Doucet," in *Architectural Theory Review*, Vol. 22, no. 1 (March 2018): 1–15.

10
Didier Debaise and Isabelle Stengers, "The Insistence of Possibles: Towards a Speculative Pragmatism," originally published as "L'insistance des possibles. Pour un pragmatisme spéculatif," *Multitudes*, no. 65 (April 2016): 82–89. Translated by Angela Brewer, https://parsejournal.com/wp-content/uploads/2017/10/PARSE_Issue6-TheInsistenceOfPossibility.pdf

The risk with speculation is that anything goes; as it tries to go beyond criticality, it also escapes critical parameters to judge the speculations themselves. Many contemporary speculative philosophies then become abstract games, repeating the formalist modality of modernist critique they aim to move away from. When the philosopher Alfred N. Whitehead wrote that "philosophy can exclude nothing" he did not mean that speculative thinking should become so general that it could include everything indiscriminately. Speculative thinking must start *from* and then think *with* everything an experience implies, so that the experience itself creates constraints. Experience exceeds sense perception; it includes ideas, expectations, tendencies, legacies, theories, policy proposals, austerities, choices and alternatives; it consists of the immense web of things, relationships, tendencies, unrealized potentials, and futures that shape our present. Continuing the project of Whitehead, philosopher Didier Debaise proposes the terms "speculative pragmatism" and "speculative empiricism": speculation as an intensification and articulation of certain dimensions that would otherwise be denied, disqualified and inaudible, a strengthening of the minority dimensions within our experiences.[8] "What matters are situations, not facts. And situations are stuffed with different realities and potentialities. And *that* is the material we should be working with."[9]

When we complicate or criticize the construction of truth, how do we do so responsibly and in an inclusive way, without falling into relativism? Can we divide *good* speculative facts from *bad* ones by tracing their construction and context, their ways of seeing that produce a proof? Speculation is an eminently ethical and political matter and requires being open to the consequences. To quote Whitehead: "Whatever the reasons justifying it, no idea is innocent."[10]

Textual Gestures

In line with this necessary situatedness of speculative thinking, against speculation for the sake of speculation, we decided not to reflect *on* questions around speculative facts, but to work *with* them. We invited four (performance) artists who work with performativity in spoken and written language to each propose a workshop in response to the fact-checkers' e-mail exchange.

Our experiment was based on the observation of a specific type of art practice that speculates with language. Within such practices, existing (theoretical) texts were not used as inspiration or justification only, but were also entrusted with the position of the protagonist, and subsequently developed further in (yet) unknown directions by using performative manipulations. Whereas today there may still be some suspense, or even (fertile) friction—for example in the relationship between languages, which enables an "erotics of translation"[11]

—in a few years time we may well have automatic translating devices that make every language barrier disappear. How can speculative experiments with text tackle the mechanical and uniform state of language that we might be headed towards? And how do we distinguish trivial bafflement from productive confusion within these intentionally created frictions and distortions between reader and text, and what does "productivity" mean in a speculative context? These questions were on the table while misreading, making up and pronouncing texts during the different exercises that Nicoline van Harskamp, Mette Edvardsen, Michael Portnoy, and Kate Briggs each proposed. The workshops took place at the Jan Van Eyck Academy in Maastricht and Onomatopee in Eindhoven, and are included in this publication as combined interviews and do-it, and question-it-yourself scripts. How far can you stretch a fact, what are the limits of speculation?

For her workshop, Mette Edvardsen turned the text (back) into raw material and invited the participants to create a new body of text without the impulse to create meaning or make sense. New, incomprehensible sentences were formed, yet the results often felt random and raised questions about its productivity and the relation between this new text and the old one. Yet, can, and should we, link experiments like this one and artistic research in general to such evaluation criteria?

The creation of neologisms was also part of the workshop that Michael Portnoy organized, which used absurdity as a productive force. In his exercise, Portnoy invited his participants to mine the fact-checkers text and create neologisms out of existing words; then to give them real content, by making up and performing their meaning. How do you play with this social contract of "taking as true," and what is the difference between funny randomness, and productive confusion?

Nicoline van Harskamp's first response to our invitation was to problematize the idea that "the truth speaks English." In her work, van Harskamp uses varieties of internationally spoken English to propose a future shaped by the ubiquity and constant evolution of the language, and its inevitable divergence from hegemonic norms. For her workshop, she focused on pronunciation and

11
Gayatri Spivak, "The Politics of Translation" in *Outside in the Teaching Machine* (New York: Routledge, 1993).

12
Luciana Parisi, "Conversation 2," in *Perhaps it is high time for a xeno-architecture to match*, ed. Armen Avanessian, Lietje Bauwens, Wouter De Raeve, Markus Miessen, and Alice Haddad (Berlin: Sternberg Press, 2017).

the politics within (misused) accents; how does what/how we hear, influence what/how we think? So-called "incorrect" English can just be noncompliance with English's capture in colonialist formats and standards.

Kate Briggs decided to question the dynamics between writing, (mis)reading, and thinking, referencing Edmund Burke Huey's book *The Psychology and Pedagogy of Reading*. Her workshop for this publication, *Reading is a Throwing Forward*, is a continuation of a previous project in which she used an eye-tracker to see how much you actually see when you read, i.e. how much of our received meanings are made up. Just like Edvardsen, Briggs pulls apart existing texts—a news story and a poem—in order for a new one to appear. Unlike Edvardsen, Briggs does not so completely. Her exercise, in which she creates gaps within its meaning, relates to what Luciana Parisi called "blind spots": the conscious creation, and instrumentalization, of "unknown unknowns" to enlarge our cognitive horizon. "We do not think of transcendental or metaphysical indeterminacy—the blind spot—as some kind of limit to human knowledge, but instead we look at how it precisely demarcates the point of incomputability that is, or rather should be, part of our construction of imaginaries, theories, and aesthetic practices."[12] According to Parisi, the indeterminate unknown is a fertile zone, without which it is impossible for new propositions, theories and artistic projects to arise. But whereas Edvardsen turned the whole text into one big "blind spot," Briggs was precise in measuring the blind spots' size and therefore its relation to the existing text. A blind spot should mark a relational actuality between two different points for it to become a *productive* lived spatiotemporal actuality.

Speculative Facts in Stories

Creative practitioners have often adopted an anti-fact stance yet, in this publication, we want to shed light on different attitudes to facticity that have emerged in response to our times, exploring the possible meaning of "speculative facts," by inviting practices that can help us get there.

First, it's important to state that speculative facts aren't necessarily *good*. In his article, Robert Trafford quoted George W. Bush advisor Karl Rove. Rove called a reporter part of the "reality-based community" and that "while you're studying (that) reality, we'll act again, creating other new realities, which you can study too." The old-fashioned, well-behaved fact-checker is always one step behind, subservient to the futures created by existing powers. Interacting with the legal field, Trafford's company Forensic Architecture looks at truth as something to be attained rather than deconstructed—a both new and oddly anachronistic goal for artists. Forensic Architecture has produced facts in court, according to legal definitions, but these investigations or ways of seeing cannot be contained by this one forum, there is an excess that needs to be shown in other platforms. Forensic Architecture's collective focus allowed for cross-referencing and building up knowledge and methodologies, against the usual market dictum that artists have to own and brand a unique area of inquiry. The term forensic means tracing what happened, but in methods for doing so they produce new types of (seeing) evidence and tracing causality, new simulations and narratives that we see as essentially speculative. Tort law is interesting in this regard. Unlike criminal law which is based on linear singular causality or responsibility, tort law allows for multiple relations, diffused causality, multiple and less direct responsibilities. This way of thinking therefore also approaches the notion of complicity in a different way: by diffusing accountability, it allows us to speak of structural violence, which makes it more fitting to deal with the abstractions, environmental destruction, scale and structures shaping our time.

Whereas Forensic Architecture focusses on debunking and tackling state-fictions by speculatively rebuilding trust in facts, writers from Mary Poovey to György Lukács have traced modern facts to a quantification and disciplinarity demanded by growing capitalism and subject-object divisions in which Western ontology is transfixed.[13] Insofar as the focus on facticity can be

13
We are largely working with a European definition of fact, yet there are precedents outside Western Modernity. Within some Australian Indigenous knowledges, people, ancestral beings and languages within a society are divided into complementary halves. When sacred knowledge is told, authorized speakers from one half perform it, and authorized people from the other half to verify it's done correctly. Media theorist and ethnographer Eric Michaels outlined this as a form of proto-fact-checking.

linked to a colonialist project, facts can be thought of as a means of control that suits the powerful. In his decolonial studies of Wikipedia, Achal Prabhala investigated the ways in which oral-based cultures had their "facts" erased. Prabhala's research tried to stretch the format of facts, including means such as "oral citations," but at the same time tried to avoid opening the floodgates to fake news and relativism. Ultimately, oral citations were not taken up by Wikipedia, and the format remained fixed.

Prabhala takes on the questions raised by the project, interviewing activists, academics and intellectuals on the African continent and asking where the contracts and institutions of facticity are colonialist or conservative, and where they should be held onto. Noko Makgato, who runs the organization Africa Check, explains the struggle of "sorting facts from fiction." Iolanda Pense and Heather Ford discuss how power that is exercised within the infrastructure of Wikipedia. The section ends with Ntone Edjabe, founder of *Chimurenga*, a platform whose publications include the *Chimurenga Chronic*—"a speculative, future-forward newspaper that travels back in time to re-imagine the present"—about experiences that refuse to be written in a straightforward journalistic way. The tension between the interviewees' positions is at the core of the book, on one hand safeguarding trust in existing truths and on the other hand the need for new stories and languages that allow contradictions and perspectives.

The disciplines that institute facts have long been of interest to Wolfgang Tillmans, an artist and photographer who "writes" by combining images and texts into a form of speculative narrative. In this publication, he makes associations between images as evidence in astrology, law and in medical and surveillance imagery. The grammar in Tillmans' language is that of both language's and photography's varied truth claims, which we read as sci-fi tales investigating truth without hegemony.

In line with an interest in speculative theories, it comes as no surprise that many philosophers and scholars are interested in (science-)fiction as a way to leave the beaten track of academic context and language. To remain faithful to the content of their point of departure, many speculative philosophers feel the need to embrace experimental forms of knowledge production as a fundamental part of their theoretical research. "Theory-fiction is the simulating engine of philosophy," according to Reza Negarestani, who wrote *Cyclonopedia* (2008) in the genre of philosophic horror-science fiction, which can be found on the shelf with other philosophy books, not in the fictional literature section.

Tristan Garcia categorized the story he wrote for this publication as "theory fiction." When asked about this via e-mail, he responded that the story is "definitely grounded in some kind of true love for falsehood (and falsehood isn't something you should look for, when you're writing theory...)." This attitude towards theory, and the relationship between his inner realist philosopher and writer of fiction, comes forth in the interview included in this publication, in which he admits that he has always had a problem with the modernist belief that you have to reflect on the medium itself or experiment with the medium itself. "I want to go to the object, with and through the medium, to what I want to describe or experience." The idea of blind spots for imagination also comes to the fore when he speaks about his new trilogy *The History of Suffering*. For this epos about hidden histories, Garcia collaborated with many experts to sketch a map of facts about very specific events and locations. When filling in the gaps for imagination in between these scientific and historical facts, such as the gnomial facial recognition of Jesus, the writer and philosopher is thus limited by the restrictions of reality.

Maryam Monalisa Ghavary similarly rewrites history in-between facts. She is the author of *American Letters*; several telegrams about immigrating Americans that are entirely speculative but rooted in historical facts. For this publication, she fact-checked her own letters and added in footnotes. Here Ghavari works with footnotes. Growing from their early days as *signe de renvoi* in medieval texts, footnotes have had multiple uses—including informing the church about who to burn—to their current use in situating a texts' references, one that has become so crucial in producing facticity.

Federico Campagna searches for the structures beneath belief. For many critics, that would be ideology. For Campagna, underneath ideology there is yet another structuring system at play: Metaphysics. Here he sketches out one possible metaphysics, a cosmology full of angels and intuitions, devils and demons (figures that were needed to produce Descartes and Maxwell's theories) opening up an intensely aesthetic approach to the underlying structures in the making of truth.

Ingo Niermann writes of knowledge as an active thing, something in which we can achieve freedom through drills that encompass habit, learning, and thinking about how we choose to make truths.

Like the performative practices many theorists, artists and writers have adopted, graphic design can also be a drill, adding pressure and stretching our habitual methodologies when we read and make meaning. Design sets the scene like architecture, orientating the readers before the text is even read. Are we at an academic lecture, or a basement sit-in, or at our mailbox receiving a letter from the government? And is the visual social contract to suspend disbelief or invest belief? A mis-oriented reader can easily read conspiracies as news, for example. How much authority do we give to the look of words, and how do the organizations that produce facts present their work? We've included a few in this book: a *New York Times* slogan, logos for Bellingcat and WikiAfrica. (Wikipedia, by the way, uses the font Arial, therefore we use it too.) In Michael Portnoy and Tristan Garcia's texts fictional books and new concepts are produced. To these we add visual typographic identities. We thought of the identities like TV shows, building an imaginary studio space around the ideas. Some were produced with a logo generator, where you pick visual stereotypes that situate a reader quickly, though our choice of style is not always straightforward. Fake news, despite its sometimes speculative quality relies on fast language and a low degree of ambiguity, while productive confusion proposes an unknown type of reading experience.

In one of the workshops, the idea of "desirable difficulty" in typography emerged. It sounded familiar to us. Difficult Times is this book's major typeface, developed by Ronja Andersen, which intervenes in the classic Times font. Parts of the font are swapped, mirrored and turned upside down. The shapes trigger one's memory. It looks like Times—the reliable design staple that delivers our news—but also not. This familiarity and estrangement creates a space to reconsider how you produce meaning when reading. The design starts off with a tightly designed system of rules, and as the book progresses it mutates and produces stranger iterations. In stages of performance, transcription, editing and design, existing logics and lines of causality are overthrown, scripts for future scenographies are made. These layers add mutation, interference, or obscuration, depending on how you see it.

The Department of Speculative Facts connects two seemingly contradictory fields of thought: what happens when we think a fact *through* and *with* speculation, and speculation *through* facts? The neologism "speculative facts" gained meaning through the reactions it provoked, in a series of stages that each drew on the last. As such, the project itself functioned as a hyperstition, or speculative fact. The Department of Speculative Facts became invested in the experiences and cultural conditions from where facts originate, and the futures they enabled. From this perspective, no idea, book or position is innocent. We have been searching for a balance between speculative proposals and positions that would (re)build trust in facts from the ground, between critically evaluating alternative scenarios and languages and letting go of a (fake) sense of control. This publication is a next step in that trajectory.

Robert Trafford FORENSIC ARCHITECTURE

Facts on the Ground

Until recently, a certain set of social and political conditions had endured which allowed us (perhaps naively) to feel secure in our relationship with truth; in the midst of these conditions, questions like "*what is a fact?*" had been consigned to the realm of philosophical abstraction, far removed from mainstream public discourse.

But for some time now, the notion of a "fact" has been simultaneously weaponized and eroded. Assumptions about the outer limits of agreed truth have been punctured and erased, largely by and for the purposes of a broad strain of authoritarian populism which is at once new and worryingly old. A philosophical concern as old as philosophy itself—*how can we be sure of what we know?*—has been repurposed for the ideological battleground of the post-internet era. The *constructedness* of facts, their function as reflections of power, was already a topic for various twentieth century theories of knowledge. But new rules of mass communication, new technological possibilities, and a new political playing field have dragged that *constructedness* into the mainstream, in ways that our existing social-political consensus has so far proved entirely unable to respond to.

It is in part these new rules that have made necessary the work of Forensic Architecture (FA), the University of London-based research agency of which I am a member. I joined Forensic Architecture from a nascent journalistic career, itself born out of time spent as an activist in France and Greece during the early throes of Europe's "refugee crisis" in 2015. There, I felt already a disconnect between what was tangibly *the case*, the facts *on the ground*, and the way those circumstances were acknowledged, or not, by bureaucracies and populations at a distance; how that distance enabled apparently fundamental obligations—the content of international treaties, for example—to be ignored.

This distance is not new, of course, and neither is its abuse. But the means by which information traverses those distances have changed, and were already changing at that time. Those changes have upended our previous assumptions about facts, and our traditional practices of truth-construction.

Forensic Architecture's researchers take as their subject matter human rights violations suffered by communities and individuals at the hands of states and their institutions. Routinely, the focus of our attention is not only acts of physical violence against individuals, but a persistent and enduring violence against evidence, by which institutions of state—police, military, or intelligence—seek to deny or minimize their actions, often by abusing the habitual trust placed in them by society-at-large. In response, Forensic Architecture (FA) proposes and performs new methods of fact-construction that might prove more resilient.

When the state is itself connected to a crime or violation of human rights, evidence may be distorted in public pronouncements to protect or justify impunity for its institutions and agents. Unchallenged, such statements stand a good chance of forming the basis of the historical record. In these cases, FA works to marry the situated experience of communities exposed to violence with the remote technical analysis of open source investigators, academics, and experts, to assemble positions that oppose the content of those government statements. At the same time, this practice of knowledge exchange, and of solidarity across borders and disciplines, assembles communities of action around these counter-positions.

A Crisis of Trust

In my training, I imbibed a fairly traditional journalistic understanding of truth as something extant *out there*, to be reached, found, and returned with. But the crisis that has recently engulfed our political and social order is essentially (though not only) a failure of faith in that model. Statistics bear out this truth: insofar as we ever did, we no longer trust institutions—state agencies, political parties, universities, newspapers, those which used to construct the world for us out of *closed sources*—to reach out into the world beyond our immediate experience and return to us with the facts. The old relationship between citizen and truth, mediated through government or journalism, was in essence vertical, a top-down relationship between authority (political, social, intellectual) and individual. But that relationship no longer holds.

The hegemony of social media has done much to precipitate this collapse, replacing the old, vertical modes of information-sharing with a dizzyingly horizontal interconnectedness. This interconnectedness in turn fosters an impression that the realm of our immediate experience has expanded dramatically, and undermines the exclusive access to information outside of our immediate purview, which was long the preserve of governments, correspondents, institutions, and academics. Against the sheer scale and vibrant promise of the open source internet, the old models of truth-production appear slow at best, fraudulent at worst.

These changes have empowered a populist relativism which has successfully cast truth as the preserve of the political and cultural elite, antithetical to various nationalist and nativist projects, and it is under the cover of this pernicious relativism that the human rights violations of the twenty-first century are carried out, and concealed.

There is a positive story to be told here, too. It is this same information revolution which has empowered the pioneers of open source intelligence, or "OSINT," among them ourselves, and our friends and partners at bell¿ngcat, Airwars, and elsewhere. The technological developments that have exploded the stability of our political systems have at the same time unlocked new avenues in civil society's enduring pursuit of accountability and transparency on the part of states and militaries around the world.

At Forensic Architecture, I quickly saw the strength of these new possibilities. The first major case on which I worked investigated allegations of illegal detention, torture, and extrajudicial killing at a military facility in northern Cameroon. According to Amnesty International, civilians were being swept up in their government's war against the Boko Haram terrorist group, detained to meet arrest targets, and tortured for information they did not have.[1]

Notably, some of those witnesses described seeing "white people" moving around the site, including within sight of the cells in which those witnesses were held. Our investigation

1 "Cameroon: Right cause, wrong means: human rights violated and justice denied in Cameroon's fight against Boko Haram," *Amnesty International* (July 2016). https://www.amnesty.org/en/documents/afr17/4260/2016/en/

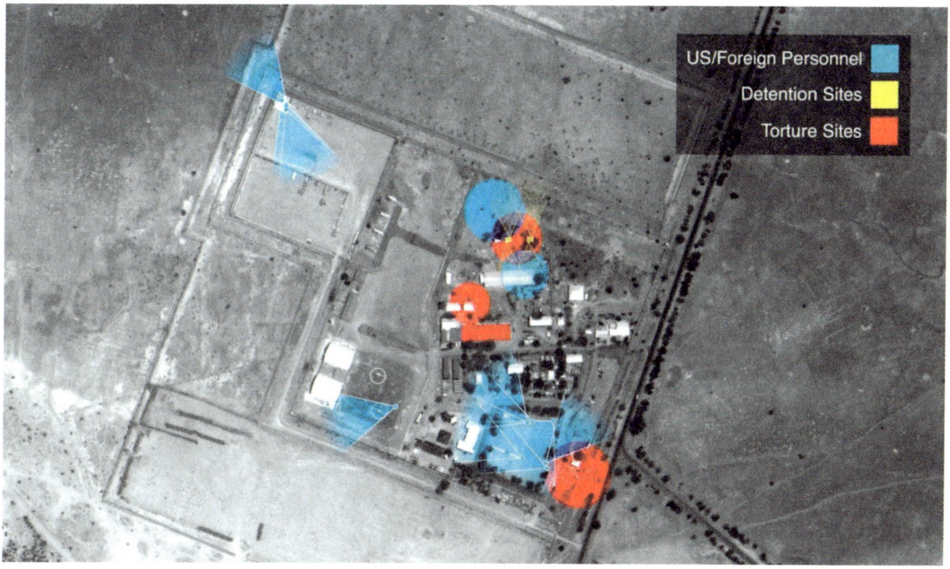

An illustrated satellite image of the Salak military facility near Maroua, northern Cameroon, the subject of a 2017 investigation by Forensic Architecture. Alleged sites of torture are marked in red; known locations of U.S. personnel in blue; and alleged sites of detention in yellow.

of this claim was a textbook example of the possibilities of open source investigation: using material that was accessible to any internet user, we connected U.S. Special Forces to the site. This connection ultimately led to the temporary suspension of U.S. military aid to the country, an internal inquiry by the U.S. Army, and the removal of a dozen or more civilians from illegal detention.

Other stories based on open source investigations have seen Russian spies expelled from Europe, and war crimes charges issued by the ICC. Social media platforms have revolutionized human rights reporting by creating the possibility for citizens to share photo and video evidence directly from conflict zones, to be analyzed by researchers around the world.

But as the internet has made investigators out of us all, traps are laid everywhere for the incautious. The new rules of mass communication have seen citizens increasingly get their news not through journalism, but through social media platforms, the economic logic of which assigns no value to truth.[2] As such, our shared understanding of, and engagement with, the world *out there* is increasingly determined by algorithmic processes of content provision, designed to recognize similarity, but entirely blind to truthfulness; at once innocent and utterly destructive.

In this way, social media has accelerated a disintegration of shared reality which has been a project of a certain strand of the political right since before the internet. There is a well-worn quote, attributed in 2004 to Karl Rove, an advisor to George W. Bush, by the journalist Ron Suskind. Suskind recalls being scorned by Rove for his "judicious study of discernible reality." Reporters like him, Rove said, were part of the "reality-based community," already fighting a losing battle against the pioneers of post-truth: "While you're studying that reality," Rove went on, "we'll act again, creating other new realities, which you can study too."

Philosophy distinguishes between "brute" facts, such as the distance from the earth to the sun, and "institutional" facts, such as the value of money. Perhaps we can understand Rove's position toward "reality"—and indeed "realities"—as an attempt to subsume brute facts, the *facts on the ground*, within institutional facts: those "facts" which are "factual" only insofar as anyone is invested in them. When all facts are framed as institutional facts, an audience is free to believe one, rather than another. In this light, the project of Rove and his ideological heirs is one of unmooring political positions from their relation to external, verifiable realities, offering its audience instead a menu of "alternative facts."

2 "Half of people now get their news from social media," *Ofcom*, 24 July 24, 2019, accessed April 21, 2020, https://www.ofcom.org.uk/about-ofcom/latest/features-and-news/half-of-people-get-news-from-social-media; Peter Suciu, "More Americans Are Getting Their News From Social Media," *Forbes*, October 11, 2019, accessed April 21, 2020, https://www.forbes.com/sites/petersuciu/2019/10/11/more-americans-are-getting-their-news-from-social-media/

It may be no coincidence that this project of the political right built its strength during the high-watermark years of transatlantic neoliberal economic consensus. Perhaps, just as (per Mark Fisher's analysis of "capitalist realism") the end of the twentieth century saw us forgetting that any other economic model was viable, or indeed desirable, we also forgot that truths might be durably constructed or meaningfully imparted by any other means than the fiat of various institutional establishments. The arrival of social media showed us otherwise, the transatlantic political earthquakes of 2016 finally exploding the myth of an information ecosystem in which *on the ground* reality could be distinguished from institutional facts. Here in the U.K., while the result of the "Brexit" referendum was undoubtedly surprising, what was, on reflection, more alarming, and more indicative of our present crisis, was the inability of the political, economic, and social hegemony of the preceding two decades to understand the emergent political language games, or to argue convincingly for itself according to their new rules.

Even after the warnings of 2016, Silicon Valley has responded slowly, limitedly, to the tangible damage wrought by social media to our political systems and social fabrics. To date, Google's total outlay to its flagship fact-checking partner is a little over $250,000. In recent years, Facebook and Twitter both declined to remove adverts from their pages that promote false claims about political candidates. Their reticence, and the raw, little-understood power of their platforms, have left space for the political performance art embraced by Rove's inheritors.

As a result, for users of those platforms, reality is now constructed out of what is persuasive, and what is shared, rather than what is true; facts have become a function of networks, of community, of in-crowds and out-crowds.

Where state propaganda once operated by abusing one's faith in institutional authority, in the social media age, misinformation travels peer-to-peer, fine-tuned and propagated by a process of digital, un-natural selection.

In this context, the conscious and attentive construction of an audience is as necessary as the construction of a fact, since the conditions which have undermined our understanding of truth have also fragmented the venues in which those facts are presented and discussed, replacing them with forums whose rules are obscured, or indeed as yet unwritten.

FA's work has long provided a model for such a practice. In 2016, the agency's researchers traveled to Israel's northern Negev desert, to the 'unrecognized' Palestinian Bedouin village of al-Araqib, which had been demolished and rebuilt over one hundred times. In order to evidence the 'residents' enduring inhabitation of the area, the team deployed a method of DIY land survey in which digital cameras were hung from simple, shop-bought kites, and flown by residents of the village, to document patterns of land use.

An FA researcher and residents of the Palestinian Bedouin village of al-Araqib fly a kite in January 2016. Together, FA and the villagers used kites such as these, mounted with cameras, to evidence their historic and continued inhabitation of the region, in the face of dispossession by the Israeli state. Photo: Ariel Caine / Forensic Architecture

That data came together with historical aerial imagery, maps, and archaeological surveys to challenge the Israeli state's assertion that the villagers were recent immigrants to the region. In fact, as we could show, their habitation of the land predated the founding of Israel in 1948.

That evidence was first presented to a truth commission organized between FA, the villagers, and a local NGO. In this community forum, not only was the evidence itself presented, but also the technical processes by which that evidence was gathered and constructed.

It is this kind of practice which makes it possible to argue for a distinction between the "constructedness" of certain facts and positions, as reflecting the effort to analyze, investigate, corroborate, and cross-reference certain claims about the world, and the cynical post-truth discourse of Rove's successors.

Open Verification and Community-based Reality

Perhaps the correct response to Rove, then, is to reclaim the notion that our realities are constructed. If our present moment of crisis has dramatically underscored the *createdness* of facts, and if truth has become a function of our (largely online) social networks, we are left with little option but to constructively embrace that entanglement. In Forensic Architecture's casework, facts emerge *out of* community, out of a coalition of voices each speaking toward a shared reality. Each voice is partial, describing aspects of that reality, but what those voices construct together approaches completeness, and in the act of mutual construction, each voice protects and amplifies the others. That understanding is at the heart of a practice that our director has termed "open verification":

> [Open verification] relies upon the creation of a community of practice in which the production of an investigation is socialized; a relation between people who experience violence, activists who take their side, [and] a diffused network of open-source investigators, scientists and other experts.

Rather, open verification proposes that civil society engage in its own transparent process of manufacture; where the processes of closed-source truth-production drew their authority from institutional reputation, the strength of open verification is in showing its working.

The "reality-based community" finds itself outflanked, checkmated; a fresh approach is urgently required. In gathering together the voices of witnesses, activists, lawyers, artists, journalists, scientists, and scholars, arranging those voices in coalition, and amplifying the picture of reality which grows out of that coalition, Forensic Architecture is engaged in constructing something like a community-based reality.

Whether it is the situated knowledge of an eyewitness or activist, the technical analysis of an expert, historical context, information from social media, or the analysis of environmental data, each contribution shines light on one part of a shared reality. Moments of synchronicity between disciplines become acts of mutual reinforcement, of construction, and what is constructed is something like a "minimum viable truth."

As Alexa Koenig, director of UC Berkeley's Human Rights Center told a conference recently: "having more voices and perspectives... helps us to build a faith in facts that we sorely need."[3] The facts are not the only thing that is built;

3 360/OS Summit, London (2019).

the *faith* in those facts must be built too. It is not enough to present evidence; the presentation of evidence must also demonstrate why *this evidence* is worthy of faith; why it should be considered convincing.

During our investigation in Cameroon, the claims of witnesses were confirmed by photographs from social media, which were in turn supported by publicly available federal contracts. We could not be certain that individual U.S. personnel knew of the crimes taking place in the buildings that they passed on their morning run. But a *minimum truth* could be established: torture and extrajudicial killings were taking place in areas which were visible and accessible to U.S. personnel.

In 2019, in partnership with the Chicago-based Invisible Institute, Forensic Architecture investigated the killing of a black man, Harith Augustus, by police in the city's South Shore neighborhood. Officers noticed Augustus carrying a firearm—Illinois is a "concealed carry" state—and asked him to stop. Less than a minute later, he was dead, shot five times. A statement by police later described the incident as an "armed confrontation," and claimed that Augustus' death was the result of a "split-second" decision, thereby justified and legitimate.

This simple contention—that its officers had acted reasonably in response to an immediate threat to their lives—was reported widely, and could have stood forever as the fact of the matter. In response, the agency's counter-investigation would constitute the construction of a complex and multipolar reality.

Comparing publicly available footage of the officers' actions to the police department's guidelines identified grave and repeated departures from protocol. Activists in South Shore attested to the inexperience of a number of the (mostly white) officers, and spoke to a history of police violence, including the killing of a black teenager five years earlier (for which a police officer was convicted of murder, and jailed.)

Consulting with a leading neuroscientist at King's College, London, we identified further contravention of the guidelines by which officers are trained to manage the use of force.

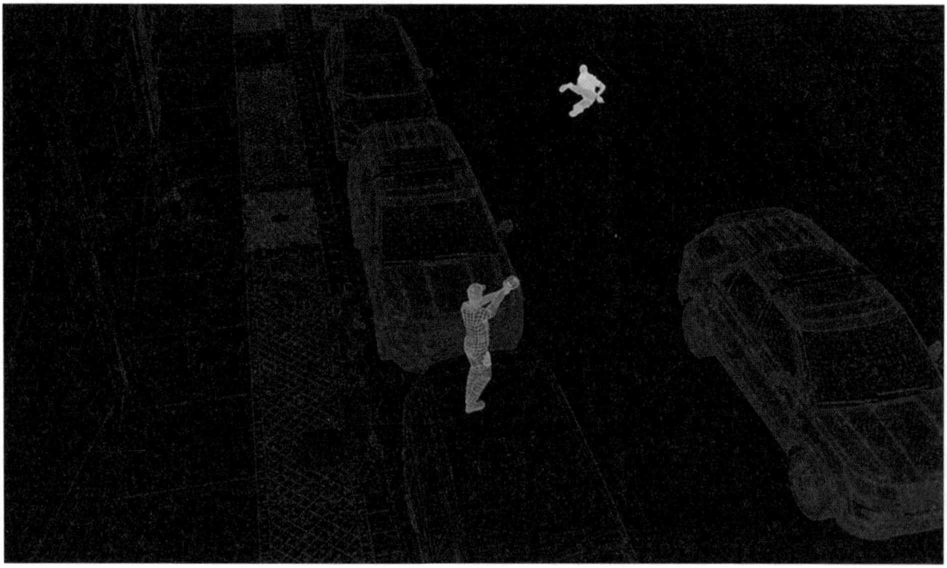

The scene in South Shore, Chicago, at the moment officer Dillon Halley fired a fifth shot at Harith Augustus, who had already collapsed to the ground. (Image: Forensic Architecture)

The agency's own video analysis revealed that from the moment he was apprehended until the moment he died, Augustus' firearm never left its holster, where it had remained securely fastened—exposing the department's description of the event as an "armed confrontation" as a deceit. In fact, the only thing in his hand at the moment Augustus died was the card that identified him as a licensed gun owner.

In the face of these technical, theoretical, and situated knowledges, intermingled and underwritten by one another, the contention of the police department quickly unraveled.

Lines of Resistance

The philosopher Umberto Eco describes external "facts" as "lines of resistance." These "lines of resistance" are out there in the world, Eco writes, waiting to "render some of our approaches fruitless."[4] They are basic instances of *this*, *not that*, upon contact with which the real value of a given interpretation of the world is revealed. Those lines cannot always outline for us what *is* the case, but they can at least tell us what is not; when a certain proposition or statement does not accord with the world of shared experience. We could understand the project outlined here as the effort to find those lines of resistance, the pieces of reality which together constitute the rebuttal of a state's lies.

In 2019, Forensic Architecture was commissioned to investigate the 2011 killing of Mark Duggan by London's Metropolitan Police. That killing, and the ways in which police distorted the truth in the days after, and minimized and ignored the demands of the victim's family, became the spark which ignited a four-day period of nationwide social unrest and rioting. A further five people were killed, over three thousand were arrested, and almost two thousand years of prison sentences handed down, but the death that began it all was never entirely understood.

Duggan had been traveling through Tottenham, north London, in a taxi. In a box next to Duggan as the vehicle was stopped was a converted blank-firing pistol. Armed police stopped the car, Duggan attempted to flee, and the nearest officer to him, apparently seeing a gun in his right hand, fired twice, killing Duggan near-instantly.

4 Umberto Eco. "Some Remarks on a New Realism." Presented at the XXIII *World Congress of Philosophy, Athens, 2013*. https://nuovorealismo.files.wordpress.com/2012/12/eco_wcp.pdf

In the minutes after his death, however, the gun was nowhere to be seen; it was eventually found seven meters away from where Duggan had been standing. The officer who fired the shots would give several statements in the years that followed, always insisting upon two seemingly contradictory propositions: first, Duggan was holding a gun in his hand. Second, he did not observe Duggan making any kind of throwing action. He could not account for the final location of the gun: "It would clear a hell of a lot of stuff up," he told a coroner's inquest in 2013, "if I was able to say 'Yes, I saw the gun fly through the air and it landed wherever.' But I didn't see it."

Years later, the U.K.'s police watchdog would conclude that the "most plausible" explanation for the location of the weapon was that Duggan had been in the process of throwing it as he was shot. As our investigation demonstrated, however, this conclusion collapses on contact with a constellation of spatial and biomechanical facts.

The officer was no more than three meters from Duggan when he fired, and was by his own admission looking directly and attentively at him, on a sunny afternoon in early August. The weight of the gun and the distance traveled being known, it is possible to determine the amount of energy necessary to convey the gun to its resting place. A U.S.-based biomechanics expert described the approximate physical movement that this would require, which we recreated within a digital model of the incident. (For good measure, our researchers traveled to the scene of the killing and attempted the throw themselves, a bag of sugar standing in for the weapon.)

Within our digital model of the scene of Mark Duggan's killing, the audience adopts the perspective of the officer who fired the fatal shots, and the throwing action necessary to carry the gun to its resting place is simulated. Image: Forensic Architecture.

The required throw is sweeping, and ends with the right arm fully extended, well away from the body: it is implausible that the officer could have missed it. Further, the officer's first shot went through Duggan's right bicep on a trajectory which suggests that his arm was by his side at the moment of the shot (as, indeed, the officer claimed it was). Even the IPCC's own forensic pathologist considered it unlikely that, following such an injury, Duggan could have made the required throw.

In each case, following the deaths of Augustus and Duggan, the public was presented with a fiction; a pernicious interpretation of the world *out there*. In Chicago, it had been an "armed confrontation"; in London, police sources told reporters that Duggan was killed after an "exchange of fire"—though not a shred of DNA evidence connected him to the gun. There is a self-defeating, circular quality to any such presentation. By the logic of state which sustains it, a police body cannot describe itself as having acted outside the law, and so the press conference, and the "facts" proposed therein, are necessarily hollowed-out, a description of an event which, like Baudrillard's Gulf War, did not occur.

What permits these interpretations to crystallize into fact? We might understand it as an absence of these "lines of resistance." That is not to say that resistance to violence and racism on the part of police forces is not practiced where that violence and racism is felt. Rather, it is to say that the routes by which such characterizations and fact-constructions are transmitted from press conference, to press, to a recipient public and widespread acceptance, are in large part well-established, unthinking, and automatic. In London, Chicago, and Cameroon, the evidence which disproved the official statements was indeed *out there*, known to some, and waiting to be held up against those claims it had the capacity to refute.

Facts and Their Audience

This points to a certain contingency: a fact can be a fact *somewhere*, while it is not yet a fact *everywhere*. Under the old models of centralized truth-production, the relationship between a fact and its audience was arguably more clearly delineated; as our lecturers would wistfully recall in journalism school, in the U.K. of the 1980s, half a dozen newspapers each had a circulation of over one million per day. The collapse of a paying customer base for print news has hollowed out this particular means of distribution, and it is at least in part this economic reality that turns reporters into stenographers, reproducing the words of police officers uncritically under time pressure and with limited resources.

Forensic Architecture has also demonstrated, to me as to many others, the success with which other forums besides traditional media can be deployed as vehicles for the dissemination of situated knowledge. Our investigation into the Duggan case was originally commissioned by lawyers representing the victim's family; the intended audience for our results was a U.K. courtroom. Through those lawyers we encountered a legal object known as a "notice to admit facts"; essentially a demand that certain statements are agreed to by both sides in a dispute, and henceforth considered "factual." Even in the spaces where a society's formal, institutional record of *what occurred* is established, the process begins with the contours of reality subject to admission and negotiation, ontologically subsequent to agreement between invested parties.

In the end, the case settled before trial, and so we took our findings instead to Tottenham, North London, and presented them for the first time less than a mile from the site of the shooting. In attendance were members of the Duggan family, relatives of other civilians killed by police in the U.K., community activists, lawyers, and local residents. What was being presented was not only the *result* of our investigation, but the very possibility of achieving that result; both the fact, and the fact-construction, were on display. Not only was the event moving, and powerfully invigorating, but it demonstrated the possibility and efficacy of new forms of dissemination, smaller, but much richer, than the pages of a national newspaper. (Though our findings were later also covered in a national newspaper.)

The fictions propagated by states about violence carried out in their names are acts of power, and evidence a capacity to fly in the face of what *really happened*. But they are also interpretations, waiting to be falsified, inviting lines of resistance to impede their trajectory. Insofar as we have faith that our community-based reality cleaves more closely than such statements to what is the case, then those atomic components of a minimum viable truth, constructed from synchronicities between situated and technical knowledges, are the building blocks of our lines of resistance. For Eco, they are "the closest we can get to truth. There is something in reality that decrees: 'No, you cannot say this.'"[5]

5 Ibid.

But where the matter at hand is civil society's resistance to violence and violations at the hands of a state, facts must also create communities of audience around themselves, in turn constructing a community-based reality. Indeed, the Latin root of "coalition," a word which so often appears in our practice, means, literally, *to grow together*. The construction of a network of mutually-supporting facts to oppose the manipulations of state institutions is also the construction of a constellation of people and organizations to invest their faith in that network of facts, and advocate for it. Facts and their audience become mutually reinforcing.

One aspect of the populist-authoritarian project is the destruction of the public commons, and the "possibility of common ground." For this reason, the fight for shared truth cannot separate the question of *what is a fact* from the question of where, and to who, that fact will be presented, and on whose behalf it will fight.

I am proud and privileged to be part of the collective of Forensic Architecture. I'm deeply grateful to Eyal Weizman, founder and director, Christina Varvia, deputy director, and everybody in the team for their daily inspiration on subjects touched upon here, and plenty of others.

Achal Prabhala

From Facts to Speculation Four Conversations

Noko Makgato AFRICA CHECK

Iolanda Pensa WIKIAFRICA

Heather Ford FACT FACTORIES

Ntone Edjabe CHIMURENGA

In 2010, I felt compelled to do something about the fact that the worlds I lived in were inconsequential to the world at large. I lived and worked—and still do—in India, Brazil and South Africa. My favorite revolutionary project, Wikipedia, did not seem to care or want to do anything about the problem, so I took things into my own hands and asked a fairly simple question: What would knowledge look like if it did not only come from books?

The answer to that question came in the form of the Oral Citations project.[1] It briefly lit up social media, was breezily dismissed by stern Dutch Wikipedians, and eventually fell down the well of good things we'd really, really, like to do but just can't get to right now. Ten years later, I am still enraged on the occasion I remember that problem, and that it still exists. Wikipedia has quietly survived the great social media backlash of the last few years. As it will continue to. Taking on Wikipedia at a time when Facebook is paving the way for despots, dictators and authoritarian populists the world over is a fool's errand: even to me, it feels like a betrayal of the resistance.

It also feels increasingly right-wing. Questioning mainstream claims, expanding sources, disputing the totality of organized western news, providing alternative analyses on things we think we know; these positions are the bedrock of alt-right social media—fake news. Or the basis of the Oral Citations project. It doesn't feel nice. It doesn't feel *fair*.

One thing I know is that this neo-conservative wave of resistance to established knowledge has firmly excluded the people, places and things that Wikipedia excluded since inception. Now, in the swirl of confusion, Wikipedia only has more reasons to justify what it is. Alt-right is here to stay, but alt-anything-else, or even plain old brown, black, gender and transgender? Class and caste? Not a chance. The house always wins. It's an internecine struggle right at the top, a factional squabble so perverse that it's almost wonderful: not even alt-knowledge can escape the grasp of the pale white male.

1 "Research: Oral Citations," Wikimedia, July 22, 2018, accessed August 17, 2020, https://meta.wikimedia.org/wiki/Research:Oral_Citations

In this speculation on the state of the fact, I turned to four people for four very different perspectives on the perils and the possibilities. For Noko Makgato, false claims constitute a clear and present danger. In Iolanda Pensa's digital journey, she has gained respect and love for the seemingly impenetrable fortress of individuals and ideologies that make Wikipedia; she knows how to snatch the keys and move in. Heather Ford offers a remarkably original perspective on how Wikipedia makes new worlds, by finding that it doesn't merely reflect the one at large—it also refracts it, casting new shapes and patterns back into our physical reality. And finally, Ntone Edjabe blows it all up by demolishing the idea that the lack of an archive, which is to say, the absence of documented fact, is a constraint. He takes this lack as liberation; using public dialogue to summon a range of experiences, memories, intuitions and unexpected forms, with deliberate slowness, to create another kind of fact—the sentimental essence of the indescribable event.

Achal Prabhala in conversation with

Noko Makgato AFRICA CHECK

Noko Makgato is the Executive Director of Africa Check,[1] a fact-checking organization that operates in South Africa, Senegal, Kenya and Nigeria.

1 "Home," *Africa Check: Sorting Fact From Fiction*, accessed August 17, 2020, https://africacheck.org

Achal Prabhala: Can you tell us a little about your journey through Africa Check?

Noko Makgato: Africa Check officially started in October of 2012. It filled a gap that existed within African journalism—of looking at the claims made on a day-to-day basis by the political elite on the continent. Fact-checking, of course, had been around for a while in the US and Europe. I was trained as a journalist, and worked mainly for financial publications in South Africa. Through my experience in that environment, and knowing how the sausage is made, I could see why fact-checking was necessary. Journalism is a difficult job, and verifying facts on a daily basis is not always possible for a number of reasons. What interested me in Africa Check, was to have the resources and the time and space to zero in on specific claims that could have the ability to impact the daily lives of people.

A: Tell us a little about Africa Check; how many countries do you work in, and how many major corrections do you issue on a daily basis?

N: We operate in four African countries, Kenya, South Africa, Senegal and Nigeria. We try to focus on countries with some degree of media freedom within their constitutions, so we can have an actual impact. In other places, fact-checking might be a noble exercise, but it would not work.

Our editorial teams over the last eight years have fact-checked over 1,500 claims. We have grown rapidly since 2016 and that's in part because of a recognized need for fact-checking on the continent.

Each claim can take between a couple of hours to a couple of days to check, as it is sometimes hard for us to gather credible data. It is a lot easier when we have authorized institutions that produce data, such as Statistics South Africa the Statistician General's Office in Nigeria.

A: How do you choose which facts to check? You have facts coming in from multiple sources, some regulated (organized television and print media) and then you have informal sources, such as WhatsApp groups, rumors and the like. How do you decide on what needs to be checked?

N: One of the factors is the potential to cause harm, either physical or societal harm. Another one is the exponential threat that comes with virality; the more people see something, the more effect it has. By the way, we don't refer to claims we check as facts, we refer to them as claims until we have checked them.

We check claims made on any platform, as long as the platform is visible for the general public. However, the claim has to be a claim, which is to say that it must be more than someone expressing an opinion.

A: What politicians say in public speeches is also in your ambit, right?

N: We particularly look at what figures of authority say and elections do indeed keep us very busy because a lot of statements are made to get support and votes. During those periods, we often unpack the manifestos that political parties release ahead of their campaigns. If the ruling party claims to have built 200,000 houses over the last six months, that's something we can sink our teeth into. It is indeed important for us who the person making the claim is, rather than just checking every statement that's being made.

A: I remember you had a partnership with a television channel in South Africa during the last elections.

N: We partner with media companies in all of the countries we operate in, because it gives us a broader reach and extends our impact. We've had partnerships with television channels like ENCA and print publications like City Press in South Africa.

A: In your work, can you recall a case across any of the four countries, where your fact-checking had a significant impact?

N: I think one specific recent example may be from the South African elections of last year. We have been fact-checking in South Africa since 2012, and we started in the other countries much later—Senegal in 2015, then Kenya and Nigeria in 2016. We measure our impact by the way authorities or public personalities are changing their own behavior because of us, that is, taking ownership for, and sharing evidence of, the claims they make in public. Last year, for the first time, the ruling party made a public announcement during the elections to encourage citizens to go and see our work and verify the claims they made.

Another party—I can't tell you which one but you can guess—reached out to us before the elections asking us to fact-check their manifesto. This is usually not at all a service we offer to political parties, but the fact that they were coming to us signified the importance of our work and how highly regarded we have become. For years, this party had completely ignored us and pretended we didn't exist. So for them to come to us and take us seriously as a key player in the information ecosystem, felt like a big acknowledgment.

Another example is the work we're doing in Nigeria. We've started a collaborative approach to fact-checking particularly on health issues. That has brought us to new kinds of information from communities that don't have access to online platforms We work with media organizations, health authorities, policymakers and there is a WhatsApp group that allows health workers on the ground to share the information they're hearing from their patients. When a doctor somewhere in remote Nigeria for example tells us of a rare disease that's emerging, we can share this story with the CDC in Nigeria, and, after verification, report back to the doctor. This is quite significant for us, as it allows us to reach people who are not on social media.

A: What is the difference between fact-checking in a rich country like the US and a poor country, like India, where I live, or any of the countries in which you work?

N: Fact-checking across the world assumes that the whole world is online and that everybody receives their information through online platforms. This is our biggest complexity; it's not that way here, and that's why we partner with media organizations, because a lot of people still get their news from television, still listen to the radio.

You asked earlier how we check claims. Most of our work comes from what people ask us to do. But our challenge is to also reach people who live in the offline world. In the countries we work in, sometimes half the population—or more—does not have access to the work we produce.

A: Do you see yourself, in the future, as an organization that services intermediaries, that is, other media organizations—or do you see yourself increasing servicing citizens directly?

N: Of course, we may impact media organizations on the way, but we don't see them as our core constituency. One of the ideas we have is to set up shops directly within communities, where people can just walk in and tell us what they're seeing and hearing. Ultimately, we are serving the widest possible public audience, and as such we would like to move to a system that functions more like a post office.

Achal Prabhala in conversation with

Iolanda Pensa WIKIAFRICA

Iolanda Pensa is a researcher, art critic and Wikipedian,[1] who lives in Italy and works in Switzerland; she is a Senior Researcher at the University of Applied Sciences and Arts of Southern Switzerland, and has worked with Wikipedians in several countries on the African continent.

1 "Iolanda Pensa," *iopensi.it*, accessed August 17, 2020, https://iopensa.it/iolanda-pensa

Wiki Africa W

Achal Prabhala: What's your history with Wikipedia?

Iolanda Pensa: I started looking at Wikipedia because I was preparing an issue of a magazine, *Africa e Mediterraneo*, on contemporary African art, specifically public art in Douala. I was interested in a historiography of this concept, and I decided to create a bibliography by inviting researchers to add to the article on African art via Italian Wikipedia. Because even though this was not a niche subject—Douala is a major city in the world—the information was not easily available, so I thought Wikipedia was the best place to define some of these subjects.

A: What were the articles with which you had the hardest time on Wikipedia?

I: One of our main tasks was to create source content, and license it correctly to make it open and usable. The other job was creating the articles. Wikipedia is like a plant; we first needed to have articles around art, in order to add articles on a particular artist. We had to build the branches. We realized that Wikipedia is very nationalistic; to encourage articles on a national subject, we needed to find national sources and they organize many competitions around heritage like Wiki Loves Monuments.[2]

A: Most sources on Wikipedia are, like all the traditional media we know and use, closed sources. So why did you create open-content sources with Creative Commons licenses?

I: We needed to create a base for the multiple sources that we had compiled about public art in Douala. We were trying to grow the plant, and one of the branches was a set of sources. Now, we have the Internet Archive and it's easier to find multiple local sources, but back then, we worked with content especially to enrich articles on Wikipedia.

2 "Wiki Loves Monuments," *Wikipedia*, accessed August 17, 2020, https://en.wikipedia.org/wiki/Wiki_Loves_Monuments

A: I'm fascinated by this idea, because so many acceptable sources on Wikipedia are to purely offline works, which means they're not instantly verifiable. I wonder whether the luxury of such citations was available to you, when working on articles related to the African continent?

I: My reputation allows others to trust me, and if I would introduce an offline citation, this might be better accepted than if someone else did. For WikiAfrica, we tried to dissociate the project with the actual writing of articles. We either produced new content offline and uploaded it, or we involved institutions who uploaded new content, like images or reviews.

A: This is a good time to talk about what WikiAfrica is.

I: The Moleskine Foundation, which was previously called Lettera27 after the missing letter in the alphabet, referring to the knowledge that is left out, funded WikiAfrica as a communications campaign for inclusive knowledge. It was very poetic and visionary, but also very complicated. What does it mean to increase African knowledge? When I arrived, they were focusing on articles in Italian Wikipedia, adding content related to African topics. It was not my cup of tea. I was more interested in how general-use articles could be more international, and include representations of experiences on the African continent, along with other perspectives.

A: What would you say were your biggest hurdles in creating Wikipedia articles on contemporary African art? Was it notability?

I: We don't agree on this, I did not find notability to be an issue at all! I found that my biggest hurdle was in fact producing sources, compiling them and using them as a base to create articles. I consider Wikipedia to be a post-colonial tool, and believe in the intention of Wikipedians—they just need to know how to do it. One of the problems is that we've never done anything like this before. We can't just replicate the post-colonial world on Wikipedia; we have to make it happen. In reality, it's not clear how we can combine all these perspectives, all these pieces in the world, in a balanced way.

A: What's an example of something you did that "trained" Wikipedia to adapt to new knowledge, or new forms of knowledge?

I: The possibility of creating indirect edits is important to me. I'm interested in getting people to work on Wikipedia by working outside of the Wikipedia community, by going offline into the real world and soliciting edits there. One way to do this is through the creation of open, accessible, source materials. Another way is to vet people from outside Wikipedia to review articles. So then, we posted their contributions to the Wikipedia page, acknowledging the people we consulted, and often the suggestions proposed were accepted by other online editors (even though the suggestions had originally been offline) and finally affected the Wikipedia article in the way we wanted.

A: Within Wikipedia, I have found that the intellectual atmosphere is somewhat constrained. How do you, as someone interested in art, speculation and theory, navigate? What is your take on the potential for imagination, especially for new knowledge in a new world, on Wikipedia?

I: I think change is a spiral movement, it is not something static. You need to exercise the muscle constantly. Wikipedia, for me, was an opportunity to create this change. It might not be revolutionary or drastic, but I think it is not impossible to scale change and make it visible on Wikipedia. There are people who have forked, who have been constrained by Wikipedia and decided to do their own thing. [Note: "Forking" is a way to split a sub-project within Wikipedia and continue it outside Wikipedia, especially when the direction of the project is not something other Wikipedians support.] But if you can stay on Wikipedia, and make the muscle work, that is the most fun, crazy and rewarding thing you can do.

A: Do you think that Wikipedia can only change in small steps, incrementally?

I: One of the things I like about Wikipedia is that you just need one person to make a difference. I do wonder how you can generate the domino effect, but there's no question as to the power and impact of Wikipedia. Our small intervention on contemporary African art, for example, completely changed the way people could think about it.

A: I find it fascinating how you can have such engaged critiques with the world, but find so much satisfaction on Wikipedia. I'm the opposite; there are times I'm quite happy with the world, but Wikipedia always drives me crazy. You're a genuine Wikipedian; I've tried throughout this conversation to get you to say one critical thing about Wikipedia and I've failed. What I see as limitations on Wikipedia, you see as possibilities. You have trust, and you have affection, and it's fun for you. When you're in the system like you are, with your emotions, perhaps nothing really is impossible.

I: Of course, there can be frustrations in the short run. But I've spent such a long time here, I can see how visionary some of the people are. I admire Wikipedians, especially some key people who play key roles, and who are recognized by other Wikipedians for their qualities. This is quite special, no? People who are consistent, coherent and influential, and a community supports them in continuing doing that.

Achal Prabhala in conversation with

Heather Ford FACT FACTORIES

Heather Ford is an Associate Professor at the School of Communications at the University of Technology, Sydney, where she is Head of Discipline for Digital and Social Media; she has worked extensively in the open culture movement, with a critical focus on Wikipedia.

Achal Prabhala: We've worked in parallel for years, and I'm interested in knowing where your journey with Wikipedia began. How about we start with that?

Heather Ford: I co-founded Creative Commons South Africa in 2004 with Andrew Rens, and Wikipedia was the single best example of why Creative Commons licenses were necessary. I was very excited about Wikipedia, particularly about the ways in which it could enable content development in local languages. Along with colleagues from iCommons and the African Commons Project, we ran the first ever Wikipedia Academy on the African continent. Wikipedia Academies were, I guess, what we now call edit-a-thons; workshops where people without any experience on Wikipedia were taught how to work with it.

A: And then your journey took a turn.

H: First I was a supporter of Wikipedia, but then I started to interrogate whether this was in fact the best solution for developing local knowledge. One of the formative moments for me within this transformation was when Ethan Zuckerman wrote about Makmende, a Kenyan character who Wikipedians tried to add to Wikipedia, but who was then again deleted by certain Wikipedia editors. It surprised me because I guess I had never thought of Wikipedia as a place where knowledge would be denied in that way, for not being notable. That was the moment I started looking at Wikipedia as a researcher; I attended WikiWars in Bangalore, which is among the most significant gatherings of important critics of Wikipedia.

A: How did your skepticism of Wikipedia develop?

H: I realized that I myself had been a big part of the utopian open content movement, fighting against the oppressors—traditional media and the big media industries—by putting things right on the internet. The Makmende case showed me that despite all the promise of the internet, where people all over the world could come together, there were things blocking this utopia—and those things had nothing to do with the copyright license.

A: Could you describe the broad themes of your Ph.D. thesis, and your forthcoming book: *Fact Factories* (MIT Press). What is confusing about the form of Wikipedia, and how are new authorities being created?

H: There are two ways in which people think about crowdsourced projects like Wikipedia. First of all, there is the perception that the technology that drives Wikipedia is neutral, and because it is open to crowds, everyone's biases will cancel each other out. I think that's the kind of logic that appears to make it so authoritative. The other surprise for me was that a lot of people thought the most unique thing about Wikipedia is that it's written by non-experts, and that only authorities have vested interests. Unfortunately, this isn't quite true.

When we started writing about Wikipedia, Mark Graham and I both thought that Wikipedia reaffirms existing disparities in knowledge. But I have found this idea, that Wikipedia perfectly mirrors the biases that we find in other knowledge systems like academic publishing, is not a helpful way of thinking about it.

Instead I've realized, and I'm very excited by this, is that Wikipedia is shaped as much from within as without. Although in many senses, it will reaffirm traditional sources of knowledge, it actually also refracts that in interesting and unique ways. One example that I give in my book is that Cebuano, which is one of the spoken languages in the Philippines, turns out to have a massive Wikipedia in that language. And the reason for that was that a Wikipedian built a bot[3] to translate every English article possible into Cebuano. So if you took this simplistic idea that Wikipedia just mirrors existing skews in knowledge production, then you're not getting the full picture.

Recently, Katherine Maher the Executive Director of the Wikimedia Foundation, addressed the fact that Donna Strickland did not have a Wikipedia page until after she won the Nobel Prize for Physics in 2018. Mahler responded by saying: you can't blame us, Wikipedia is just a mirror of the world's biases, not the source of them. She later however, very gracefully, acknowledged that she shouldn't have underplayed Wikipedia's own production of bias. The problem however is that this so called "neutrality"—this idea that Wikipedia merely reflects the world as it is, without bias—is an embedded logic about Wikipedia and it lets Wikipedia off the hook in fundamental ways. In my book, I'm trying to share a more nuanced understanding of how Wikipedia's own ideology, and their tools, end up shaping what can exist in Wikipedia, and deciding what can never, ever exist in those representations.

3 "Why are there so many articles in the Cebuano language on Wikipedia?" *Quora*, accessed August 17, 2020, https://www.quora.com/Why-are-there-so-many-articles-in-the-Cebuano-language-on-Wikipedia

A: This is fascinating. I want to point to some other examples of how Wikipedia is doing more than reflecting the world, but refracting it, as you put it. You have language Wikipedias that punch far above their weight—in terms of speakers—such as Catalan, Hebrew and Afrikaans. These aren't bot-generated projects; they're fueled by a fierce sense of identity. I wouldn't call this a bad thing per se, and I guess neither would you. Now you were careful in measuring your words in describing how Wikipedia can—and does—change the world as it is. Wikipedia is making a new world, and yet this world is not necessarily open to all. How to square this up?

H: I've been working with a historian to see if we can study how Wikipedia represents Australian events. I kept using the word "bias," and she responded interestingly to that term. All knowledge projects are constituted by issues of power and access, she said, and every public knowledge project has been characterized by issues of inclusion. What's important to me is the spaces that are available for people to come together and sort out their differences. I think these spaces are getting thinner and thinner on Wikipedia, if they ever existed. I'm interested in how power is exercised within Wikipedia—how, and whether, power is justified within Wikipedia through dialogue. It's about how Wikipedia represents people who might never have the power to actually edit Wikipedia. That has led me to think about how institutions might be able to help people represent themselves on platforms like Wikipedia.

A: I was speaking to Erik Möller, the former board member and Deputy Director of the Wikimedia Foundation, and he was only half-joking when he said that porn and pop-culture are the only two things where young, white, western, male editors are willing to create new knowledge, and give that knowledge a new authority. There's a lot of truth in that. Can you think of any instances where you felt a dissonance, where a new form of authority was attempted to be created that caused you to pause and think?

H: I can think of a few, but we could start with Sur; the game played in India, which came out of your project on oral citations. It was put up for deletion when translated into English, and of course, the oral citations themselves were contested on the reliable sources noticeboard. What Wikipedians think they're doing is passively reflecting authority in the world. But the policy is circular: basically, they're saying reliable sources are... reliable sources. It gives people the opportunity to make their own subjective decisions about what they feel constitutes objective knowledge. And this is what has happened through history; my knowledge is fact, yours is merely opinion. Through "reliable sources" policy, Wikipedians decide what constitutes the truth in this way.

A: And this is consequential because so much of what's on Wikipedia ends up being the basis of the internet, and therefore, the world.

H: Absolutely. I've been investigating how information on Wikipedia ends up in Google's knowledge boxes. It means that the classifications used on Wikipedia—in Egypt, during the Arab Spring, for example, whether they called it a "protest" or "revolution"—those kinds of classifications get circulated way beyond Wikipedia and get represented in everything that describes that event because no one questions the algorithm when the base of knowledge is Wikipedia.

A: One argument I have heard right since I started making trouble within Wikipedia, was that editors are simply following the rules. That Wikipedia is not exclusionary by design, but is by default, almost by mistake. That there isn't an ideology within Wikipedia. What do you do with these arguments?

H: This is the million-dollar question. I've become particularly interested in ideas of ignorance. There's willful ignorance, for instance, when people just don't want to know about certain things. And I think that the only reason there are people who can still say that Wikipedia is neutral territory is because, underpinning it, there is a system of exclusion that's an integral part of Wikipedia's infrastructure—as there is with any knowledge project that seeks to represent the world.

Achal Prabhala in conversation with

Ntone Edjabe

CHIMURENGA

Ntone Edjabe is the founder and editor of *Chimurenga*,[1] an award-winning Pan-African cultural platform for editorial and curatorial work. In this conversation, he refers to two recent projects from *Chimurenga*. The first is an account of the assassination of Congolese President Laurent-Désiré Kabila on January 16, 2001, at the Palais de Marbre in Kinshasa, called, *Who Killed Kabila?*[2] The second is an account of FESTAC '77, the festival which brought artists, writers, musicians, activists and scholars from Africa and the black diaspora to Lagos. *FESTAC '77*,[3] is the first publication to address the "planetary scale" of the festival alongside the personal and artistic encounters it made possible.

1 *Chimurenga: Who no know go know*, accessed August 17, 2020, https://chimurengachronic.co.za

2 The Chronic, "The Chronic: Who Killed Kabila," *Chimurenga*, September 19, 2019, accessed August 17, 2020, https://chimurengachronic.co.za/the-chronic-who-killed-kabila/

3 The Chronic, "FESTAC '77 BOOK – OUT NOW," *Chimurenga Library, Library Book Series, News*, January 25, 2020, accessed August 17, 2020, https://chimurengachronic.co.za/festac-77-book/

Achal Prabhala: Ntone, to begin with, you publish a range of non-fiction in *Chimurenga*, and you match that with speculative work, with fiction, with art. When you conceived of *Chimurenga*, did you conceive of it this way? As a mix of fact and speculation? Was it something you thought about?

Ntone Edjabe: From the get-go there was very much an element of us trying to find a way to tell stories that we did not have factual information about. Fact gathering can be an elite pursuit, it is what establishes a "newspaper of record" as such, for those interested in that status. We were not even going to try to write our world through those unassailable means. We had intuitions, we had memory—and by memory I mean access to people who lived through events we were trying to make sense of. I was already interested in stories that are not verifiable in the classic sense and as such the choice of music as the theme and method for the first issue was not incidental. I think music allows us to be undisciplined—to be disrespectful of categories and established modes of writing. For Lee Perry the mixing board is a musical instrument. For Fela the song is a journalism report, the band is a political party and the club is a place of worship. They stretch technology to breaking point and assimilate the possibilities it offers. The aim isn't to invent or re-invent forms. Or even to reform disciplines, or to point to their limits. This is not new, Zora Neale Hurston spoke of it as decorating the decoration, which sounds pointless and beautiful. And I doubt Amos Tutuola ever had any stake in saving journalism or the novel, he was telling complicated stories set in worlds where the dividing wall between fact and fiction isn't as rigid. And reproducing them in English from Yoruba, a language in which poetry is spoken through drums.

From the beginning, it was clear that as an editor I would privilege work that raised these questions. And in a way the *Chronic* accelerated this process—it began as a newspaper that was entirely speculative.

A: I'm interested in the effect of some of the work you've published. Especially essays like Njabulo Ndebele's writing on Brenda Fassie, the great South African singer. Here was a major intellectual writing about a pop star. What did that do?

N: The challenge was to redefine the "new" rather than focus on news, learning to write about something, someone we all "know," like Brenda. She touched us all in some way, but we don't have the language for that affect. The sense for me was that sometimes, the experience refuses to be written in a straightforward journalistic way. The event itself is plural.

In any case, to me it was less important to determine how many meters the distance between A and B is and say that it is exactly ninety-six centimeters—I am sure you know Borges's joke about "exactitude in science." I didn't particularly care about that. Rather, how do you articulate the sense of smallness or bigness of the room? What other devices do you use when you don't have a ruler to measure it or since you may have only seen it or experienced it from a particular place? And then how do you share this knowledge confidently? That is the effect I've paid most attention to, the possibility for all readers to assume an editorial role—this happens when we discuss football for example. It doesn't matter who the writer is, there is always someone who knows better! For example, an event like FESTAC involved at least 20,000 artists from all over the world, all of them radical people, artists, musicians and writers. And even though many describe it as transformative, very few of them have written about it. I was curious about what makes FESTAC unwriteable. There are several things to consider: one is the inaccessibility of facts—no one can tell for sure how many people were there, even who was there, and what took place. The event was so large that it couldn't be planned entirely top-down, all the organizers had was intense political will and lots of petro-dollars. I've looked at all the official records I could find, they all contradict each other. For instance, I know of a whole delegation from the PAC (Pan African Congress) in South Africa who landed in Nigeria without any documents—no passports, let alone visas. They are not recorded anywhere, except they claim they were guests of honor of the Nigerian governments as Soweto revolutionaries! It was an event that operated both over-ground and underground. Now whether the PAC group was nine or eleven people—even this is disputed—isn't my focus. I am immediately drawn to how their presence in Lagos complicates the story of South Africa's participation in the event, and by extension the story of the liberation struggle etc. Now all these tangents can induce paralysis, if one is trying to write the definitive history of FESTAC—until someone with enough arrogance, time and money shows up to tell your story. The aquarium is too big so we might as well describe it from inside, instead of stepping further and further back from it—the proverbial bird's eye view. And this requires different tools like speculation, rumor, imagination, memory, etc.

A: Do you feel that time is a factor that makes FESTAC unwriteable? That the significance of an event like that needs time to be properly understood?

N: Yes, time plays a role. It provides some necessary distance. But I am always trying to trick the clock—you remember that the first issue of *Chronic* was written in the present tense of 2008 from the hindsight of 2010? These are speculative tools that we can use. And again, we borrow them from music. The composer Julius Eastman often described his music as organic—meaning that each musical phrase contains elements from the previous and the next. So in a sense both the past and the future are always present in each phrase. And many of our musical traditions function in this mode. Some of our work involves transferring these methods to the realm of writing, as in the case of the first issue of *Chronic*, or even the FESTAC book, which is written in the present tense of 1977—we can write both inside and outside of time.

If you take for instance, the assassination of Kabila as a starting point, the newspapers of "record"—*El Pais*, the *New York Times*, *Le Monde*, or *Nation* in Nairobi—were all contradicting each other about what happened and they all stuck to their particular line. One paper is using the Minister of Foreign Affairs of Angola as the source. Another quotes a Congolese minister. And so forth. There are so many countries involved and with as many interests. And we know political murder generates this level of speculation. I was interested in this story because we cannot establish even basic facts—not only who killed him, but even if he is dead or alive in the days following the shooting. Even though it happened in broad daylight—1pm in the middle of Kinshasa.

Now Congolese guitarists often use a trance-inducing technique called the *sebene*—popularized by Franco Luambo in the 1960s. On the surface the sebene sounds like the guitarist is playing the same note repeatedly. In fact this is not the case, the variations are so slight that they are not perceptible to the listener, they can only be "felt" by the dancer—this is what induces the trance. The sebene opens a break in which what is heard and what is felt are both distinct and present. And they constitute a thing that is multiple—I don't mean that perspective varies from one location to the next, that is true too. But here each repeated phrase feels different to the dancer. We used this as license to produce a story that allows the contradictions to sit more comfortably together—each narrative as believable as the next.

That project was also an attempt to make sense of the war in Congo and the many rebel groups that participated in it, with shifting allegiances from one week to the next—Achille Mbembe called them "war machines." Congolese music groups usually evolve through a process called "dislocation," where the importance of a group is measured by the number of times it has splintered—in other words the afterlife of a group is as important as their actual productions. It is a process too layered to describe here, but it allows us to analyze the many splinterings among rebel groups beyond the discourse of warlords and gratuitous violence etc.

A: Some years ago, I attempted—and abandoned—a project to translate science fiction written in Telugu, a South Indian language, from 1938. A big part of what motivated me to try it was a sense of having to establish the facts of speculation: that we did it, even then. What kind of sense of pride or ownership did you bring to the FESTAC project? How does that inform your work on Fela Kuti, which is, as with FESTAC, less about the "facts" and more about the facts of feelings he generated in his lifetime and beyond?

N: Firstly, we do not have archives. Some people see this as debilitating but for me it is liberating because we can determine our own points of entry into history. We don't waste time contesting the state's version because it doesn't exist—the first thing each new head of state does is to wipe out what came before them. But we do have memory. Take a seemingly simple story like the one about the military assault at Fela's house, the Kalakuta Republic in Lagos, by the Obassanjo regime. It begins in February 1977, a week after FESTAC. Some of the facts, of course, have been established—the day and time of the assault, and there are witnesses. But the event does not stop there. To be able to describe it accurately you have to pay attention to the music—which has information that wouldn't make it to print. In song, across many songs, Fela describes the event as something that actually lasts for two years! For two whole years, he is living "inside" this event—he carries the injuries, goes in and out of jail, in and out of courts, loses his mother, his home etc. And he continually narrates this process through episodic song-writing, with no division between the event proper and its afterlife. He finally only buries the event in 1979 when he literally puts it into a coffin and takes the coffin to Obasanjo's presidential palace at Aso Rock. That is the most authentic narration of the so-called Kalakuta Massacre at our disposal—but even this is considered a conservative framing by some Lagos historians, who put the beginning of the event at 1946, with the formation of the Abeokuta Women's Union, an organization founded by Fela's mother to challenge British colonial rule.

A: That's wonderful. In an earlier conversation we had talked about how, in many parts of the world, music is the literary archive of the country.[4] Getting back to the question of time, a lot of your work is about the past. And you do that from a point in time that is without question set in the present, working with people who work in the contemporary, the now. Is that a fair assessment?

N: At the very least, I think, our work poses the question of whether the past is in fact in the past. There are familiar accusations that Africans live inside the memory of slavery, colonization, apartheid, and that we need to "move on" etc. I find this baseless, not only for the claim by people like Cheikh Anta Diop that we've been denied a past—and a future, I might add. But also because we have the creative resources to exist inside many temporalities. You can hear this in our music. Some of our best writers display this capacity—in one of the essays he wrote for the *Chronic*, about Youssou N'dour, Binyavanga Wainaina continually shifts tenses to the most thrilling effect—somehow he manages to convey the thickness of N'dour's trajectory. In *Ceddo*, a film he made in 1977, Sembene Ousmane collapses both the introduction of Christianity and Islam in West Africa into the same historical time. Then suddenly, inexplicably, shifts the narrative to the future. And for a few minutes the story set in pre-colonial Senegal comes at us from some point we have no knowledge of. Then it casually returns—no explication provided. And if you approach time from a music perspective, as rhythm or tempo, then you're no longer tied to clock-time of the event, but also the time involved in narrating the

4 "Music is the Weapon," *The Modern Magazine* no. 692 (April 2017), accessed August 17, 2020, http://www.india-seminar.com/2017/692/692_interview.htm

event. It took us at least five or six years to produce the book on FESTAC—and that was deliberate. We wanted to *take* time. And the process itself was a series of events at different speeds. Publishing can be a way of thinking about publishing. For our project on Kabila, we produced three books, en route to producing *the* book.

Our work is in present tense. It is always present tense.

FESTAC '77, published by *Chimurenga*, 2019. Photo: Department of Speculative Facts [illegible] to save [illegible] name of [illegible] between [illegible] there [illegible] sabota- [illegible] heads [illegible] postpone [illegible] liberation [illegible] because [illegible] tunes of [illegible] imperialism. [illegible] with the [illegible] masters and at [illegible] Afri- [illegible] the roof [illegible] one is [illegible] about the messa- [illegible] which is that [illegible] Africa lies [illegible] of the people [illegible] should offer [illegible] for our pre- [illegible] and that the [illegible] is to mobilise all [illegible] because the [illegible] bright.

If we could die in fore- [illegible] wars which have nothing to offer the black man, then we should be prepared to fight our own wars now. The song of freedom towards the end, carry the revolutionary

[illegible] in which African slaves are carted away [illegible] the sordid slave trade era.

[illegible] traces the [illegible] black [illegible] from [illegible] primitive [illegible] slave trade to the [illegible] independence [illegible] from 1960 [illegible] the [illegible] simplistic [illegible] Arabic and [illegible] dramatised [illegible]

fervours and nationlistic cries that African youths have no alternative than to take to arms to fight for their freedom.

The DRUM as presented by Somalia should be seen as the food for thought for all African countries, the message is loud and clear and that is that OAU is a good forum if only we can make some positive contri- butions instead of lip ser- vices which will carry us no where.

☆ ☆ ☆

The last colourful sing song and dance was the fi- nal round up as pictures of dedicated African lea- ders are shown at the back- ground—all those who be- lieve in Africa for Africans like late Dr. Kwame Nkru- mah, Cabral, and the pic- tures of Lt. General Olu- segun Obasanjo and Siad Barre of Somalia. And the final songs are in praise of FESTAC and all it sym- bolises for the black man.

The cast is made up of 20 women and some 20 odd men and all in their various ways did entertain the audience. The simpli- city of the theme and plot, the ease with which, the audience is able to un- derstand the whole perfor- mances shows that there is a lot stage plays can do to re-educate the black man so that he can liberate him- self from the shackles of foreign domination.

The DRUM by the So- mali Troupe is a didactic play that has relevance for our joint aspirations as brothers in the search for ultimate peace and free- dom. The Drum, apart from striking at the core of the FESTAC ideals, needs no further drumming before we get the message. We must wake up from our deep slumber and fight now.

The play is a good enter- tainment in terms of sin- ging and dancing but be- hind this external appeal lies the deep political mes- sage, only Africans can re- deem their sordid colonial past through their deter- mination to fight for their freedom. Now is the time.

[illegible] the neo-colonial era of middlemen [illegible] dence after we had fought and died [illegible] in a nutshell, traces the whole gamut [illegible] his seemingly primitive quiet and [illegible] days of slave trade to the era of [illegible] from 1960.

3 Somali a[illegible]

From OJO BEJIDE

THREE members of the Somali contingent to the FESTAC and a Nigerian driver died in a road acci- dent near Kontagora, Niger State, on Thursday.

Fifteen others, including six women and another Nigerian driver, were inju- red.

The contingent was travel- ling to Jos on the invitation of the Plateau State Govern- ment for a drama perfor- mance.

The bodies of the victims have been taken to the Ah- madu Bello University Hospi- tal mortuary while the in- jured passengers are on admission there also.

I saw the victims in the hospital.

One of the victims a woman, sobbed bitterly but a nurse patted her on the back and said: "Never mind you will soon be all right again."

Treatment

The Kaduna State Gover- nor, Group Captain Usman Jibrin and the Somali Minis- ter for Higher Education and Culture, Mr. Omar Arteh, had visited the victims in hospital.

The minister told Group Captain Jibrin, that he was touched by the tremendous and brotherly care and assistance given to the in- jured by the hospital and government officials.

He said one of the injur- ed had told him: "I am sa- tisfied if I should die."

-2-

AKENDENG

Britain:
anisational
was apparently unloaded and taken to the wrong place.
Police outriders guided our coach through the Lagos traffic. We were to learn later that the relatively free flow of vehicles in the city was due to a decree which allowed odd numbered vehicles on the road one day, and even numbers the next. Every-one was allowed out only on Sundays.
Lagos is a city in the process of change. There is a rash of breaking down and building everywhere.
In spite of extensive discussion, which we were later to have in the colloquium about the need to build with traditional materials

Wolfgang Tillmans
From *truth study center* (2005–ongoing) and other projects

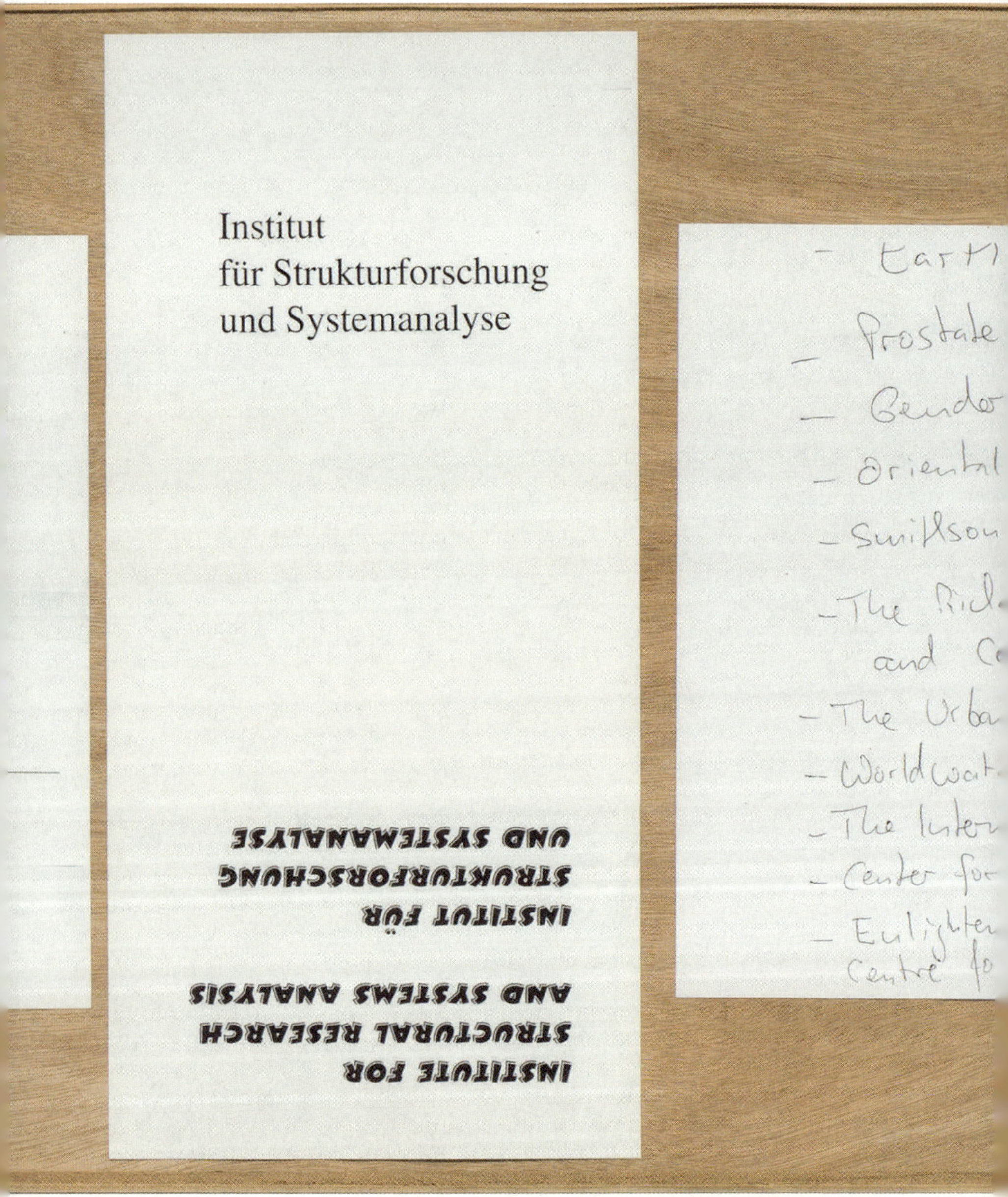
Institut
für Strukturforschung
und Systemanalyse
INSTITUT FÜR
STRUKTURFORSCHUNG
UND SYSTEMANALYSE
INSTITUTE FOR
STRUCTURAL RESEARCH
AND SYSTEMS ANALYSIS

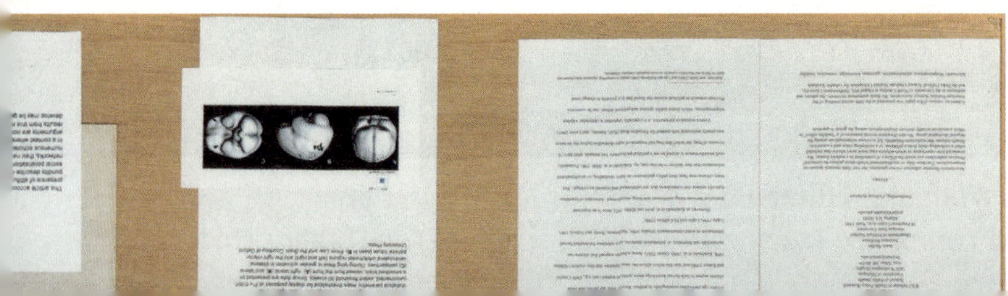

er Research Institute
itute
itute Research Archives
itution Research Information System
Institute for Peace Studies
Resolution
itute
ute Research Library
Economics Study Center
l and Renaissance Studies
cement of Enlightenment
A Compelling Documentary on the Armenian Genocide

Mbeki replied that antiretroviral nevirapine has not been registered for MTCT anywhere in the world and that the World Health Organisation is still considering its use for this purpose. "A National Steering Committee on MTCT has already met and will finalise its report mid-October," says Mbeki.

On the question whether he believes that HIV is a minor or major cause of AIDS, Mbeki replied that "there is a serious AIDS problem".

On the question of AIDS orphans, Mbeki replied that "orphans result from the health crisis in SA, caused by many diseases".

He pointed to 1999 WHO estimates of the causes of death in Africa, which stated that 12% of deaths are caused by HIV/AIDS, but heart diseases is still the biggest killer. "All these cause orphans," says Mbeki.

On the question why there is a delay in MTCT in other provinces when the Western Cape, the only province not controlled by the ANC, has successfully implemented free treatment, Mbeki replied that "This matter will be dealt with through the Steering Committee on MTCT".

On the call to go for an HIV test by PAC spokesperson Patricia de Lille, who went for a public HIV test recently to spur on other politicians to lead by example, Mbeki replied that "It is important to know what the state of one's health is - in my capacity as president of this country I go for regular health check-ups".

On the controversial debate whether HIV causes AIDS sparked by Mbeki's courting so-called AIDS dissidents in his presidential AIDS panel, Mbeki replied that "The way we have handled the complex scientific questions around HIV/AIDS may have been confusing, but there is nothing confusing about what government HIV/AIDS programmes are based on and are trying to do".

DATE: 10 September 2000
EVENT: TIME Magazine interview
SOURCE: "Gov releases parts of Time Magazine to quell Mbeki AIDS controversy." *South African Press Association*, 10 Sep 2000.

"Clearly there is such a thing as acquired immune deficiency. The question you have to ask is, what produces this deficiency?" he said.

"Now, if you go through the literature, ordinary standard literature available in medical schools, there will be a whole variety of things [that] can cause the immune system to collapse.

"Endemic poverty, the impact of nutrition, contaminated water, all of these things, will result in immune deficiency."

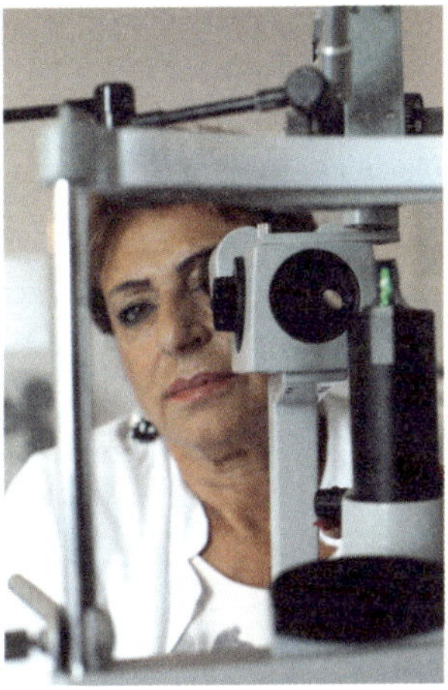

W
M

BEHAVIORAL AND BRAIN SCIENCES (2011) 34, 1–56

The evolution and psychology of self-deception

William von Hippel
School of Psychology, University of Queensland, St Lucia, QLD 4072, Australia
billvh@psy.uq.edu.au
http://www.psy.uq.edu.au/directory/index.html?id=1159

Robert Trivers
Department of Anthropology, Rutgers University, New Brunswick, NJ 08901
trivers@rci.rutgers.edu
http://anthro.rutgers.edu/
index.php?option=com_content&task=view&id=102&Itemid=136

bstract: In this article we argue that self-deception evolved to facilitate interpersonal deception by allowing people to avoid the cues conscious deception that might reveal deceptive intent. Self-deception has two additional advantages: It eliminates the costly gnitive load that is typically associated with deceiving, and it can minimize retribution if the deception is discovered. Beyond its le in specific acts of deception, self-deceptive self-enhancement also allows people to display more confidence than is warranted, hich has a host of social advantages. The question then arises of how the self can be both deceiver and deceived. We propose that is is achieved through dissociations of mental processes, including conscious versus unconscious memories, conscious versus nconscious attitudes, and automatic versus controlled processes. Given the variety of methods for deceiving others, it should come no surprise that self-deception manifests itself in a number of different psychological processes, and we discuss various types of lf-deception. We then discuss the interpersonal versus intrapersonal nature of self-deception before considering the levels of nsciousness at which the self can be deceived. Finally, we contrast our evolutionary approach to self-deception with current eories and debates in psychology and consider some of the costs associated with self-deception.

eywords: deception; evolutionary psychology; motivated cognition; self-deception; social psychology

hy would people deceive themselves? What is the mental chitecture that enables the same person to be both decei- r and deceived? How does self-deception manifest itself ychologically? And how do these three questions interre- ? In this article we address these issues with an evol- nary account of self-deception, according to which f-deception evolved to facilitate deception of others. st, we define what we mean by self-deception and scribe how self-deception serves the goal of interpersonal ception. We then discuss the non-unitary nature of the nd and how different types of psychological dualism ble the same person to be both deceiver and deceived. xt we describe different varieties of self-deception d the evidence for these different varieties. We then cuss the interpersonal versus intrapersonal nature of f-deception before considering the levels of conscious- s at which the self can be deceived. Finally, we contrast r evolutionary approach to self-deception with current ories and debates in psychology.

Deception and self-deception

ere are many ways to deceive other people. An obvious oice is to tell an outright lie, but it is also possible to ceive others by avoiding the truth, obfuscating the truth, exaggerating the truth, or casting doubt on the truth. Just as these processes are useful in deceiving others, they can also be useful in deceiving the self. For example, if I can deceive you by avoiding a critical piece of information, then it stands to reason that I can deceive myself in the same manner. Thus, we consider various types of self-deception, including biased information search strategies, biased interpretive processes, and biased memory processes. What marks all of these varieties of self-deception is that people favor welcome over unwelcome information in a manner that reflects their goals or motivations (in this sense, our approach to self-deception is consistent with Kunda 1990; Mele 1997; Pyszczynski & Greenberg 1987). We also consider classic cases of self-deception such as rationalization and convincing the self that a lie is true.

WILLIAM VON HIPPEL, professor of psychology at the University of Queensland, Australia, conducts research in social cognition and evolutionary psychology.

ROBERT TRIVERS, professor of anthropology at Rutgers University, is best known for his theories of reciprocal altruism, parental investment and sexual selection, parental control of offspring sex ratio, and parent–offspring conflict. Trivers is recipient of the Crafoord Prize for "his fundamental analysis of social evolution, conflict and cooperation."

 0140-525X/11 $40.00

Dishonesty magnitude was also greater when dishonesty served the self and the other than when it only served the self

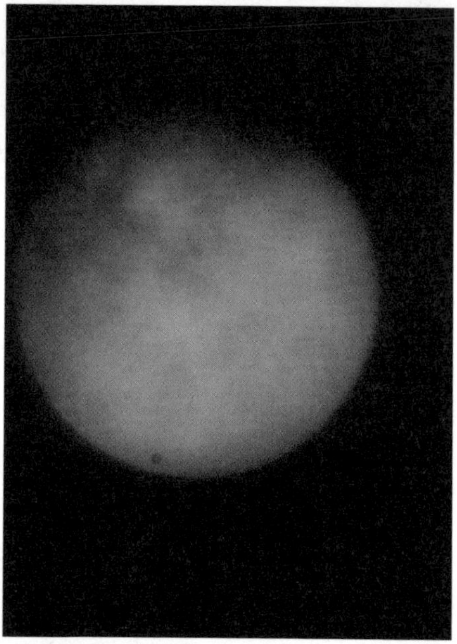
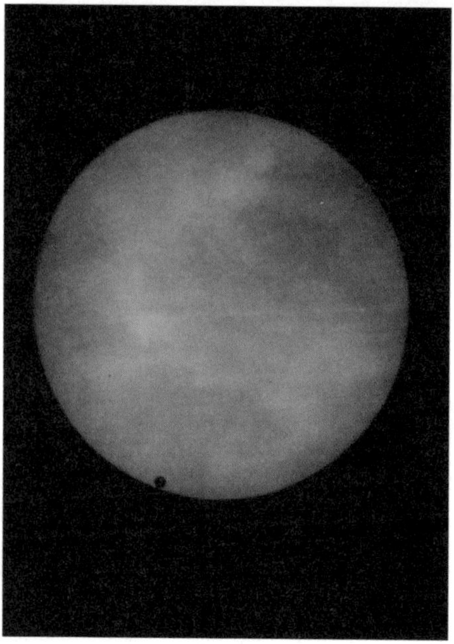

2004

A transit of Venus happens when the Sun, Venus and Earth are in perfect alignment. Observed from Earth it manifests itself as the small black disk of the planet Venus slowly wandering over the bright disk of the Sun in the course of several hours. This is an extremely rare phenomenon because the planes of the orbits of Earth and Venus are slightly tilted toeach other and a transit can only occur when both planets are exactly at the point where the planes of their orbits meet. This happens in a regular cycle of 122 years, then eight years later, after which it takes another 105 years, then again eight years and then again 122 years and so on. The last transit took place on 8 June 2004. This was also the first that any human being alive at that time on Earth could have seen. In effect, evidence of transits of Venus actually occurring has only been given through historical written reports or drawings, beginning from the time of the invention of the telescope and later through photographic images of the two transits which occurred after the invention of photography. Only six transits have been observed in human history, which were those of 1639, 1761, 1769, 187 4, 1882 and 2004.
In the 18th and 19th centuries the observation of this geometrical phenomenon had a huge scientific importance. Researchers understood that they could calculate the distance between the Earth and the Sun through the exact observation and comparison of the passage times of Venus over the disk of the sun as recorded from distant points on Earth. At that time it was considered to be the only way to more or less exactly establish our own absolute position in relation to the Sun and hence to the universe around us. Only the relative distances in our solar system were known, measured in multiples of the distance between the Earth and the Sun, not the absolute distances. It was like having a map without scale.
Various ambitious expeditions, for example Captain Cook's first one in 1769, were undertaken for the sole purpose of observing the transit of Venus from a point as far away from Europe as possible. The idea was to measure the parallax, which, in simple terms, can be described as observing the displacement of a nearer object in front of a more distant object viewed from two different points; like for example observing the changing position of a thumb held up in front of a house on the horizon alternately viewed with one or the other eye shut. The exactness of clocking the event was impaired by the black drop effect, which caused Venus' disk to be seemingly connected to the sky around the Sun for a while longer than should be expected from its predicted position. Even though it was supposed to be already clearly 'inside' the Sun's disk, Venus' disk was deformed into a drop-like shape. Only through photographic observation of the two transits of the 19th century was it established that the drop effect was actually an illusion caused by the human brain.
Observing the transit of 2004 through the telescope, which I still have from my astronomy obsessed teenage days, had of course no scientific value, but it was a moving experience to see the actual mechanics of the sky work in front of my eyes. To see a planet actually move in front of another defined object that is part of the solar system gave me as an earthbound human a visual sense of my location in space. Despite the flatness of the telescopic image one could experience space as three-dimensional space. The next transit of Venus will occur on 6 June 2012. WT (2005)

2012

How likely is it that only I am right in this matter?

Quelle est la probabilité que je sois
le seul à avoir raison à ce sujet ?

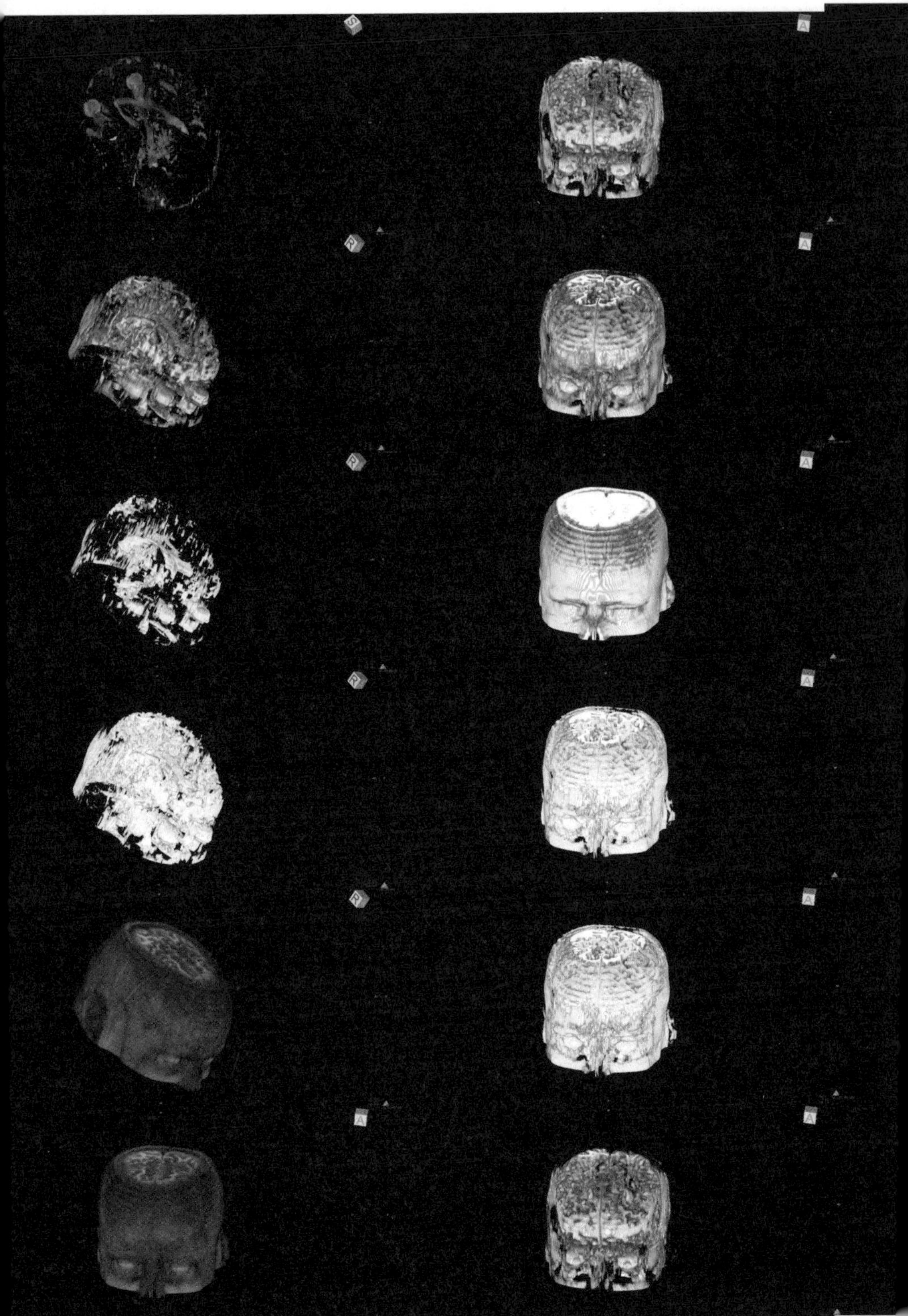

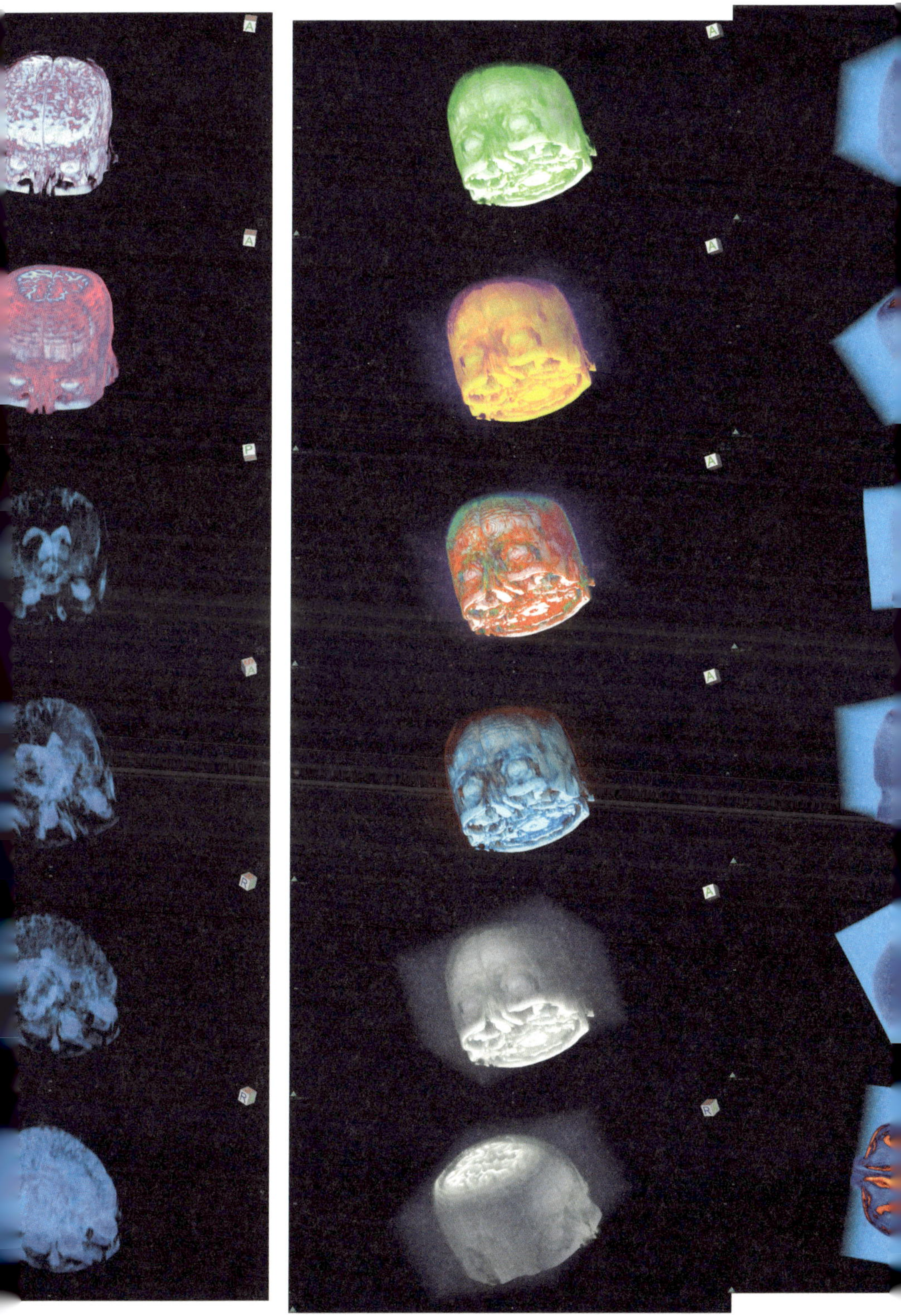

Memorial for the Victims of Organized Religions,
2005

Participants' starting dishonesty was greater when dishonesty was self-serving than when it was self-harming

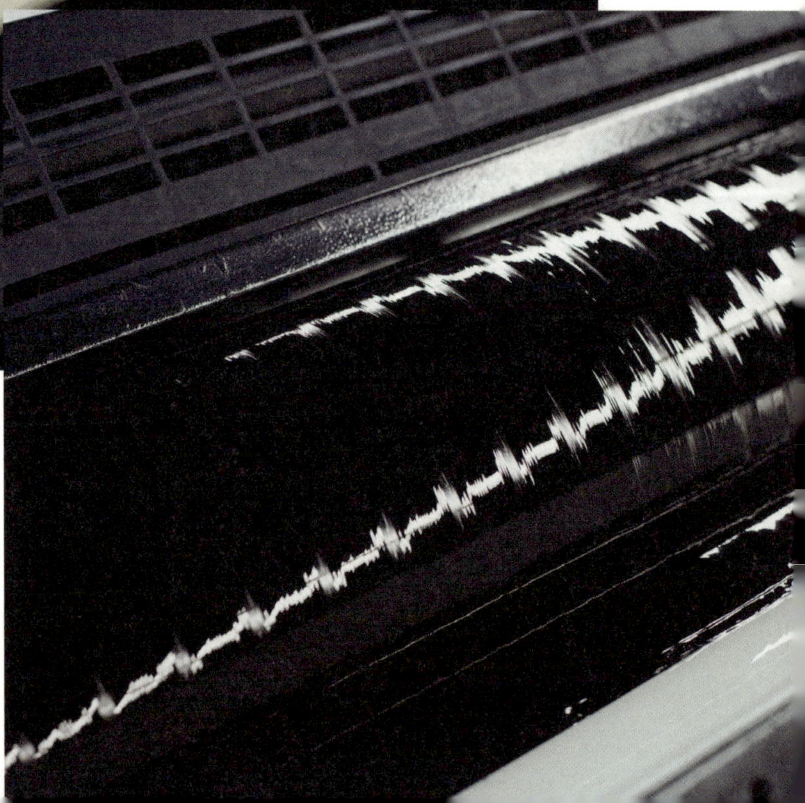

Tristan Garcia interviewed by Lietje Bauwens DOSF

Escaping Humanity

Sitting on a Parisian terrace, it feels logical to start our conversation with *Hate: A Love Story*. This novel, about the French capital during the AIDS crisis in the 1980s and the search for subversive positions within this debate, put Tristan Garcia on the map as a promising young philosopher and writer. Yet, as soon as I bring up the book, the author makes an ugly face and says: "It embarrasses me to talk about *Hate*—I wrote things I did not know enough about, with a kind of innocence that I can now only call naïve."

Lietje Bauwens: Wasn't that exactly the intention of *Hate*, starting from a critique of literary autofiction, to write about what you had *not* experienced?

Tristan Garcia: It was indeed my intention to write about a time that I had not experienced, from a perspective that was clearly not mine, but I did it in a very short-sighted way. And when the book won a lot of important literary prizes, they were presented by the writers that I so despised at that time, who were concerned with a so-called "literature of self." They celebrated that I had conceived some kind of intelligent trick; that my book was a strategic choice.

Hate's approach came from my findings while writing *Form and Object*; in which I make the metaphysical claim that "the self" is always closed to itself, that there is no self in itself; the table is not in itself as much as I am not in-myself. The conclusion I drew from this was that through the openness of the "self," I could become everything and everyone, and the only thing I could not write about was myself. As a white man of the low middle class, with a quiet and happy childhood, I always felt I was an absolutely uninteresting writing object to myself anyway. In my opinion, it is a missed opportunity to engage in literature with your own voice, reflecting on your own position within society and thus taking your own subjectivity as an object. You do not make use of fiction's possibility to vary from one's subjectivity. Around the same time, identity politics became increasingly popular. My ideas came from metaphysics, but I forgot that *Hate* was not a metaphysical book at all, but a concrete story about an existing community. And that collided.

L: Next to feeling naïve, did you also feel guilty to the LGBT community for telling "their" story?

T: I have a big problem with the presupposition within the idea of cultural appropriation that you "have" what you "are," that identity is a property which you can "take away" from someone else. Identity politics takes gender, race and identity as shared qualities which make you part of a set of individuals, of a group. By defining identity, however fluid, as "having" instead of "being," you hold on to the capitalist idea of ownership. I did nevertheless feel guilty about the people who had lived through the 1980s, who were in one way or another connected to the AIDS crisis. Many felt deprived; they found that someone who had had the disease or who had lost a loved one should have told the story. What makes me feel most uncomfortable is that I stayed true to what actually happened, and because of that I could not really say that I had just written fiction. I guess it was a mistake. The fiction was not radical enough and thus I entered dangerous territory without knowing it myself.

L: In your second book *Memoires de la Jungle* you write from the perspective of a chimpanzee who tries to become a human being. Did you solve the problems you had with *Hate* by taking the fiction a step further?

T: In *Memoires de la Jungle* I did not try to be a different gender or sexuality—I went into a completely different animal species, which made it very clear that I was writing fiction. Whereas *Hate* was a successful book that I hated myself, *Memoires de la Jungle* was ridiculed by almost all critics, but I was, and still am, very happy with it. Not in the least because it became a sort of cult fiction for people who work with monkeys.

L: How important is accuracy for you?

T: I was fascinated by experiments from the forties to the eighties in which human families took chimpanzees in their family and took care of them. These were often couples that had a baby and at the same time adopted a monkey to raise it exactly the same way, with the same clothes, rules, etc. This mostly went well until a certain age, when the human child started to talk while the monkey of course did not. From that moment on, a hierarchical relationship arose and the human child started to act against his non-human brother or sister. All of the experiments had a tragic outcome when the chimpanzee began to feel disabled and eventually had to be taken away from his human family. There is not much information about what happened to them afterward, I only know of one case in which a chimpanzee was sent back to his chimpanzee family but was no longer welcome there. He was not human enough for the human world, yet too human to go back to his so-called "nature." I have always been interested and really touched by this "in-between space" because it reminds me of my own position as a writer; I too always try to go outside of myself, but at the same time I can never completely become someone else.

The book confronted me with the limits of my own language and form of life, the way I perceive and experience the world. When I wrote *Memoirs*, I no longer had the naïve idea that I could become a monkey, at the same time, precisely because of this failure, I was able to understand the failure of a chimpanzee who tries to become a human being, but who also fails to escape his own species. The book marked a very short moment in which I experienced the limits of my humanity.

L: Can you also be a monkey, or another non-human being, that does not try to be a human being?

T: If I try to be a tree through literary language, this does not mean that that tree also wants to become me. The only thing we have in common is that the tree is also not in itself, but in the world. I really liked the poem by Henri Michaux *Magic: Part 1* where he makes a lot of effort to become an apple, and if he finally succeeds, he finds out that the apple was never in the apple and that "entering an apple" means to be thrown out in the outside—and then he suddenly lies on the table. For me, trying to become something or someone else, is a way to enter into the world.

L: What role can language play here?

T: I do not like a glorification of literature, in which literature is taken as something divine or sacred. Language is not absolute because it is human. When we use language, verbs and adjectives, we relate to the limits of our perception of the world. If we want to move to a non-human perspective, we cannot keep using our own language and syntax. At the same time, language should not be seen as a sign of human finitude, but rather an access to the outside world.

L: As a writer, how do you alienate yourself from yourself, into (the direction of) another (non-human) perspective?

T: What I call the "immanence of the point of view" is important here; how do you write completely from the perspective of the person who experiences it, without describing the outside of the subject like some sort of "omniscient" writer? It took me years to know enough about chimpanzees to actually "become" one. For example, chimpanzees are very exhausting when you meet them for the first time, it seems like they run around the same way, and make the same movements all the time. Until you notice that they are introducing small variations, like sometimes running slightly softer and taking on different rhythms. You start to notice a difference in the "cycle of sameness." When writing the book,

I tried to reproduce that by, for example, often repeating and reversing a sentence, each time with a small difference—"this is in that, and that is outside of this and this is within that." Via language I could experiment with a life that is not linear but circular and inclusive of small differentiations. A simpler example is that chimpanzees are smaller than humans, which means that their field of vision is different. In order to get their perspective, I wrote every chapter and decor first from my own point of view, to then take a meter off. As a result, from the eyes of the chimpanzee certain things are suddenly higher or even completely out of view.

L: So you don't work with neologisms, or the creation of new unknown word combinations, as has been done much within literature and poetry.

T: I know many interesting literary experiments with new languages, such as the Zaum of Klebnikov, some parts of *Finnegans Wake*, or glossolalias by Antonin Artaud, but I have always had a problem with the modernist belief that you have to reflect on, or experiment with, the medium itself. I want to go to the object, with and through the medium, to what I want to describe or experience.

The value of this experiment lies precisely in the confrontation with the limits of our own (linguistic) capabilities. Of course, the language of the chimpanzee is a bit experimental. For a while now, three different writers have been working on translating the book, but it just doesn't seem possible. This actually seems fitting; the book tries to escape its "Frenchness," but is caught in it.

L: Your book *Âmes* (souls) the first part of *Histoire de la Souffrance*, is an epic; the (world) history of suffering. Why did you choose the form of an epic?

T: This is the book I've been training for, I feel like I first had to write six other books before I could write a book of this proportion. In *The History of Suffering* everything that I've been experimenting with over the past years comes together: animals, plants, people, historical research, science fiction and contemporary realism.

I did not want to write an epic about humanity, but an epic about life on earth; against the postmodern idea that big stories are dead and also beyond the limits of individual human lives. Of course, the whole idea of an epic, an imperialistic story about victory and thus humiliation, is very problematic. *The Iliad* and *Odyssey* are basically descriptions of genocides, and modern epics as for example written by Victor Hugo, are in a way humiliations of the old world through celebrating the victory of enlightenment ideals. How to hold on to the form of an epic, without humiliating any (form of) life? I wanted to write an epic of forgotten stories, of histories that have never been given a place within historical consciousness. This epic describes the general history of suffering from the perspectives of women, slaves, disabled and sick people and animals. The first book starts before suffering, and describes what a worm (according to current studies the first organism with brain function) being chopped in two feels. This is pure suffering, because suffering means life that is separated from itself.

L: The complete epic is about four transmigrating souls that each time embody something or someone else throughout history; like a tree, a Korean girl during the Buddhafication of Japan and even Jesus. What does the soul, and its religious connotation, mean to you?

T: As a philosopher, I have never been religious and do not believe in the soul. As a writer however, I think that the material soul is the subject of literature. A story actually tries to capture a subjectivity through its actions in time, and I think this is exactly what the soul was for religion. There are very interesting studies of stories about religious judgment in ancient Egypt or Mesopotamia where a God awaits dead people to judge their lives. What information do you need for this judgment? A photo is a snapshot in which you cannot possibly catch an entire "being"; and so you have to tell a story. Your soul is that story; it does not contain everything you have ever done or said but it is a selection of your actions. It is a character or essence that is not timeless, as in many metaphysical views such as Plato's *Eidos*, but time-bound. In literature, you are dealing with a soul because you write a character without a visual appearance, it is only in letters on paper, and it is not timeless because in your writing you connect it to a certain moment.

L: In a way you rewrite history, from the position of a fiction writer. You have clearly done a lot of historical research, but there still is little information available about those forgotten pieces that you are interested in. How did you deal with these (imperialist) restrictions?

T: I have worked on this book for ten years and every chapter, however short, is actually a book in itself because of all the research that was needed. For each chapter I collaborated with experts, who I call mentors, to learn as much as possible about, for example, a period in the Middle Ages, crusades of lepers and extinct population groups. I spoke with the last Ngadjadjara expert (an endangered group of Aboriginals from Australia) about how an Australian person, who had never seen a lion, would observe and describe it. For the conversation between Jesus and the other crucified, I worked together with the Jesus Seminar, an intellectual project in which 200 theologians gathered each year between 1985 and 2005 for historical-linguistic readings from the Bible.

The basis of the epic is therefore collective and I could not have written this book without the internet; if you use only books and written sources for your research, you are limited to information about and from the West.

L: And then, after all this research, you are left with gaps—the spaces in which imagination can operate. How do fiction and reality relate to each other in *The History of Suffering*? Do you feel a responsibility to be transparent about when you are "historically or scientifically accurate" and when you are fictionalizing events?

T: Through gnomic facial reconstructions we know now, for example, what Jesus looked like; that he wasn't white-skinned, we know the shape of his face. These are hypothetical facts, grounded in contemporary research, that I stick to when I write. I am not a postmodernist; I do not occupy myself too long with subjective representation and different layers of meaning. My conception of realism is that something is less or more realistic. I want to switch to the role of philosopher again here, because years ago I worked a lot on the notion of representation, specifically within photography. For example, even when you have a very realistic photo of a dog, it is not entirely impossible to see a cat in it. The more realistic the picture, the harder it becomes to make things up. The stories I tell are never completely realistic, but I let myself be limited by the restrictions of reality.

The idea of my epic is that I want to describe an event-less history, beyond the great historical events. But whereas centuries ago it was still possible to find gaps in between the big events, everything has now become much more packed. Nowadays everything is an event, there are almost no in-between spaces in the twenty-first century to locate my souls in.

Another big blind spot is the end of the series, when suffering and thus life ceases. Can the matter that remains remember that there once was life, or does it take life to be able to think itself? As a philosopher, I shall defend a metaphysical position—everything that once was, will always be present in more or less intense way—but as a writer I am not yet sure…

L: You have been separating the writer and the philosopher often in this conversation. How do these two relate for you, and within you, to each other?

T: When I started writing both fiction and philosophy, my greatest fear was to write philosophical literature or literary fiction. This is a well-known phenomenon in France, think for example of Sartre. The problem with philosophical literature is that you only work out ideas, instead of creating characters and souls. You hold on to the world of concepts, which results in a sort of monolithic, didactic work of art. Yet I also really did not want to write literary philosophy like Derrida, Bataille and Blanchot, who actually wanted to be poets. In order to escape all of the literary and semiotic theory that occurred in philosophy during my studies, I was particularly attracted to analytical philosophy and formal logic (not anymore, I must say!).

My way of doing both things was to agree with myself that as a writer I would always oppose the philosopher, and vice versa.

L: Oppositions are at the core of *La Vie Intense* in which you write about the continuous yet impossible tendency to reduce life and thinking to each other.

T: As a dualist I hold on to a separation between thinking and living. But to remain faithful to duality, I also make a distinction between the way in which the two are separated. When you think, you have to separate the thinking from living; you cannot pretend that to think is the same as to live, that it's possible to embody thought. From the perspective of living, however, thinking and living are part of the same flow, which can be more or less intense. As a living person, you experience the continuity between life and thinking, simply because we cannot alienate ourselves from our thinking.

In line with this separation between life and thinking, I use literature and fiction to explore the variety of different lives and philosophy to accelerate abstractions. Where literature exists by the grace of qualities and details, philosophy wants to get rid of all specific colors and scents. This acceleration of abstraction, looking for a world without properties, is very important but it also gives you something very poor in return that as a writer I have absolutely no interest in.

L: Especially *Nous* seems to contradict your fictional writing. It argues that the bigger the "community," the weaker its shared ground, while in your literature you are always concerned with stretching empathic abilities.

T: One of the main spearheads of progressive thought is that subjectivity must be stretched so that animals, plants and so on can fit in, in *Nous* I argue that with this extension you lose a certain intensity of the common ground. That to me is the failure of progress. By collecting more in the picture, you lose focus, the "we" becomes broader and broader but also weaker and weaker because contradictions that were first external are now being brought in.

So here the writer and the philosopher are indeed on opposite sides. In the *History of Suffering* I have tried to connect as many people and things as possible in one large network of objects—the philosopher in me would say that I dug my own grave doing that.

A Dutch version of this interview appeared in *nY39 magazine*, 2019.

Ingo Niermann

On Learning

The common way that biological creatures learn, in so-called implicit or unconscious learning, is through repetition. Repetition reinforces the importance of an action or perception and puts it to the test at the same time. The former is necessary as a prioritization (finite creatures can't perceive or do everything), the latter as situations always turn out a bit differently. Through repetition we both learn to asymptotically abstract general rules (induction) and apply them as habits (deduction). Everything that we do and perceive trains some of our generalizations. Similar to evolution, implicit learning is a gradual process. Stability out-weighs speed and perfection. Only exceptionally intense experiences make us learn instantly—under shock. When we are unable to unlearn, even though later experiences put the lessons learned under shock into question, then we have incurred a trauma.

As an additional tool, our episodic memory allows us to retrospectively construct or to re-evaluate existing rules. This so-called explicit learning builds up our semantic memory. In order to not stress ourselves with abrupt changes and to learn to apply the rules they only become effective through repeated deliberate testing, i.e. training. As soon as we are able to smoothly apply a rule we internalize it; i.e. apply it implicitly. Deliberately applying a rule often enough that it no longer has to be deliberately applied is called instrumental conditioning. Instrumental conditioning appropriates implicit learning through repetition until it becomes accepted as if learned implicitly.

Discipline is the act of steadily applying a rule without the intention for it to be internalized. Dry training is a form of explicit learning that saves us and others from any damages as long as we don't exercise a rule properly. To make dry learning entertaining, we can design it as a game. A school instructs and supervises you in dry learning. A dare is the opposite of dry training as it trains you in taking—real—risks. A dry training that prepares for a dare is a drill. Every drill turns into a dare as soon as you internalize it and no longer need discipline to repeat it.

While even just the task of consciously observing what has been learned implicitly can distract us to the degree that we temporarily forget about it, explicit, i.e. conscious, learning is often understood as intelligence in a narrower sense. But phenomena like priming or sudden inspiration show to what degree our explicit thinking is controlled unconsciously. Every time we remember we are implicitly manipulating our memory to bring it more in line with our old and new, explicit and implicit generalizations—not to speak of what we just don't remember or forget forever. Sudden intellectual progress occurs often after we have been sleeping or absent-minded.

Most of the learning of children is completely implicit: they still have a lot to learn to catch up with adults (implicitly copying them) and their brains still allow them to learn easily within genetic pre-configurations (from walking to speaking). Their explicit memory is still rather weak—both of concrete events (episodic memory) as of general knowledge (semantic memory). Playing is less of a deliberate practice of dry training and amusement than an implicit setting.

Philosophy and sciences have long ignored implicit learning. Even after acknowledging that we are largely controlled by unconscious motives and habits they commonly assumed that learning and thereby overcoming our natural instincts happens only consciously. At best, after some time passes, this knowledge would be internalized. This explicit-to-implicit learning has been condemned as stupid learning, like that of the Pavlovian dog. Although there's a substantial difference between our explicit-to-implicit learning and that of the Pavlovian dog (at least how it used to be perceived by science); thanks to our episodic and semantic memory we don't (completely) forget how the learning started and what we have assumed to learn. When the bell doesn't deliver food, we can still recapture why it is that we produce saliva.

At a very young age, when our explicit memory is hardly evolved, we start to become indoctrinated with commonsensical philosophical concepts, such as those of spirits and souls. As soon as we are able to reflect on these concepts we easily overlook the importance of implicit learning as we are unaware of it, unless we exercise it with full intention. While the hubris of our consciousness to do it all alone constrains our individuality and helps to naturalize our cultural predispositions.

Confusion about the character of our consciousness culminates in the concept of free will. Studies show that the moment we consciously decide on a physical action our brain is already in preparation for it. Some philosophers and scientists have concluded that consciousness is just a sort of accidental epiphenomenon without casual power. But we can reflect on our consciousness and leave traces, like this text. Others have called the concept of free will a vain illusion that is at the same time fundamental for our social and personal responsibility. But where does the intuition of a free will come from—even against our beliefs? (It's so much easier to stop believing in gods, spirits or eternal souls.)

Even if free will exists, it doesn't necessarily translate into free action—a discrepancy known as the intention-behavior gap. Our consciousness is less steering than supervising. Besides, this supervision is manipulated and often bears only mediate results. When it comes to our autonomic nervous system, we cannot consciously influence it at all.

The reason that we tend to overestimate our conscious capacities is not just from a misleading concept of our mind but the fact that everyday life rarely puts them to the test. Most of the time we are consciously in line or brought into line with our implicit reactions. Or we don't even have the time to realize that we didn't have the time to question them. All that there is usually left to do is to retrospectively make sense of our implicit decisions, i.e. rationalize them. Our explicit thinking is too slow and too limited to interfere comprehensively with our everyday actions—only in rare cases of strong opposition is it just fast enough to stop actions from really beginning.

Our implicit thinking has been demonized as a lava of emotions, ridiculed as an atavistic, biased set of tools from the stone age or adored as a source of eternal wisdom though different from our explicit thinking it is constantly tested and improved. In the last years, we have been flooded with scientific news about the remarkable intellectual capacities of other animals in the use of tools, abstract thinking, or self-awareness.

Often these discoveries are interpreted as proof that animals are equipped with explicit learning like us. But they could also be read as proof to what degree intelligence operates without explicit learning. What seems to distinguish us from other animals is less our explicit capacities than the amount of implicit rules that are not genetically or early determined (instincts and imprintings) but still flexible through our life (internalizations). A complex, rapidly transforming society tests our abilities of constant learning to the limit. Even more it's important that, instead of using our feeble conscious capacities to futilely fight our unconscious drives, we have to expand and renew them according to our needs. This is our (relatively) unique source of change.

To explicitly induce shocks is risky and difficult to direct, so what remains in a private, amateurish context is the self-induced drill, i.e. auto drill. Only by aiming at a distant future can our free will out-rule its lagging and translate as full volition. We can drill ourselves into new routines just as much as into new feelings. Drills allow us to act more considerately or more passionately. It just takes time for each drill to come into effect and for building one drill up after another (chaining) and not to overtax us with too general or several parallel drills. Once an implicit rule is in place we can move to the next one. The more we drill ourselves the more we'll tend to drill ourselves further and further.

Implicit rules don't need us to explicitly take care. We don't even have to believe in them. They work unless we make an effort to stop them. We don't absorb and frustrate our tiny bit of awareness with futile self-control but reserve it for new challenges, ideas and joys. Drills don't cheat, but they give up on belief and honesty as constantly explicit acts. To move safely you don't have to keep all your body on the ground; you can also walk, run or jump, i.e. fall forward in a controlled form. And, once you have learned those techniques properly, you are even safer as they make you more versatile than when sticking to the ground.

But is it worth the effort to wait till skills become implicit? Why should we learn to walk when tomorrow we might already be able to fly or live underwater? Why should we learn how to navigate in one area when tomorrow we might already move to the next? Why should we make an effort to train ourselves when soon we can easily reprogram ourselves in no time? Computers and robots will allow us to act magically upon, i.e. perfectly enslave, the world and ourselves.

In its beginnings, artificial intelligence has been modeled as an ideal realization of flawless explicit learning: computers forget nothing and conclude and implement their learnings in no time. This happened not only because of an overestimation of the importance of explicit learning but because humans' conscious capacities are so limited that it didn't take much computational power to outdo them in many ways. Only when it comes to figuring out rules by themselves is this approach insufficient. For this, artificial intelligence has to be equipped also with implicit learning, i.e. gradual adaptation through repetition.

Meanwhile, computers can't just count but can also adapt so fast and on so many layers, i.e. learn so "deep," that we have difficulties to comprehend them—even more than we have difficulties to comprehend our own unconsciousness. To be able to read software directly also implies the possibility to manipulate it directly, and big data undermines its own predictions. In contrast, drills make us reliable to ourselves and others. That's why drills have been a crucial tool of collective indoctrination—and will be so even more in a future in which we are surrounded by devices that are all programmed to serve and drill us with the same sophistication. But drills can also be applied individually by ourselves and thereby turned into a tool of personal freedom. It's only our own drills that protect us against those of others.

Scripts

1. DoSF invited two fact-checkers from the *New York Times Magazine* to exchange letters about their profession.

Alex Carp & Jamie Fisher

↓

2. We handed their e-mail exchange over to four artists working with language and speculation, to organize workshops departing from these texts.

Michael Portnoy
Nicoline Van Harskamp
Mette Edvardsen
Kate Briggs

↓

3. Together with the artists, we turned the workshop events into scripts.

Alex Carp & Jamie Fisher NEW YORK TIMES MAGAZINE

Re:

From: Alex Carp
Date: Tue, Oct 23, 2018 at 12:42 PM
To: Jamie Fisher
Subject: Re:

Hi Jamie,

In a way it feels fitting that we should begin a conversation about fact-checking in a form that is a little bit manufactured, so here we go. I figure we can tell a few stories about our experiences and thoughts on fact-checking, and ask each other questions, though I imagine those should be guideposts rather than limits, and we can be a bit freewheeling as well. I know that you and I both think a lot about how fact-checking fits into the world—both the world of journalism, and the world beyond it—so we might as well start there. I know you saw the new Broadway play about a fact-checker, *The Lifespan of a Fact*, this weekend, and I'm very curious to hear more about your thoughts, especially about the public depiction and understanding of fact-checking, versus our often (but not always) more prosaic experiences of it as a day job. How did the play compare?

Also, a question I wonder about it: Why would anyone go see it?! My wife and some of my friends have asked me if I want to go see it, and until very recently I found myself sort of repelled. (Though now I think I might as well, or at least when its run ends, I'll want to *have* seen it.) I guess I worry that the job itself would be minimized in a way, or that we'd be stereotyped as some sort of humorless arbiters of truth, whereas the most interesting parts of fact-checking for me are the moments of not knowing what the answer is, where we actually have to figure out how to get to the bottom of something, which feels a lot more like a process of feeling your way along than a simple yes/no response to if something is true or not. I don't know about you, but I got into fact-checking as a way to learn more about writing and editing, and to open up relationships with people who care about their work and are curious about the world, and so the job is only partially an end in itself. But especially as fact-checking has seemed to have a moment recently, it's made me rethink what I take from the job versus how other people, both in journalism and beyond, might see it, and what parts of my experience I sense they probably aren't seeing.

One thing the job has definitely changed for me, though, is how I read other published work—both because I'll sometimes spot a tricky detail in a deeply reported piece and wonder how they went about confirming it, and also when I'll see obvious errors or carelessness in other magazines or on websites, which for me can color everything else that publication runs. One story along these lines that stuck with me, which I long thought must be an urban legend, was the detail that Van Halen, when they were on tour, had a rider in their contract that all the brown M&Ms had to be removed from their snack bowl. Different versions of this story exist, but I had usually heard them as parables about rock star vanity or pettiness. Then I heard an episode of *This American Life* that looked into it, and it turns out that not only was it true, but it had a real purpose: Van Halen was the first band to take huge rock productions into smaller, mid-tier cities, which meant that smaller and smaller arenas needed to be set up with complicated electronic and pyrotechnic gear likely for the first time ever—and if something went wrong, it could stop the show or be really dangerous.[1] So taking out the brown M&Ms signaled to the band that all the details in their contract had been read thoroughly, and everything would be set up safely and ready to go (that the weight of the gear wouldn't sink a hole in the stage—which

Ira Glass, "They Might be Giants," *This American Life*, April 15, 2011, accessed August 12, 2020. https://www.thisamericanlife.org/433/fine-print-2011

happened, apparently—or the venue doors were too small to move the bigger equipment from the trucks to the stage). As it turns out, there's also a Snopes entry on this,[2] which has a screenshot of the actual contract! I think this story has stuck with me not only because it's about attention to detail, but also because it was a truth that people relayed sort of loosely, and once someone took the effort to get to the bottom of the story, the truth was so much more interesting, and said so much more not only about where and how two very different worlds came together, but also upends a lot of the common assumptions about arena-rock stars—especially ones followed by stories of partying and destroyed dressing rooms, etc—and the care they take with their work that the shorter, lazier version of the story played in to.

Looking forward to hearing your thoughts in a day or two.
Alex

From: Jamie Fisher
Date: Thu, Oct 25, 2018 at 11:03 AM
To: Alex Carp
Subject: Re:

Alex! Always a pleasure to talk shop with you.

I have to ask—why do you feel the artificiality of the format is fitting? I've been thinking about/overthinking your intro more than you might expect, haha. Is it because fact-checking isn't something that happens in the real world, outside magazine journalism? Is it because what we do is so oddly specific and so much more limited than an engagement with the truth? I think about what we do as engaging with the visible. We have to make sure that the statements made in the article connect with the provable world. I guess in that sense I think about fact-checking as the only real component in a genre that is inherently a little manufactured.

God, the play! Why would anyone go see it? The cynical but appreciative answer is to see Daniel Radcliffe. Now I'm really overthinking, but isn't theater a kind of fact-check for cinema? You go to see that these people who exist on screens really exist, that they exert some kind of charisma that can be felt across the stage and legitimize, in some way, their success. My straight answer is that I don't really understand the play's audience. Actual fact-checkers and Publishing Folks in general know how this

2 David Mikkelson, "Did Van Halen's Concert Contract Require the Removal of Brown M&Ms?" *Snopes* (January 19, 2001) accessed August 14, 2020, https://www.snopes.com/fact-check/brown-out/

business works, and if the goal is to educate people who don't know, the play isn't quite accurate. It was fun to watch but I felt so much excited anxiety watching it, worried that they were about to skewer us—worried less that I would be embarrassed in some way than that the lay audience would go away with a permanently skewed misconception about how fact-checking works, or what its priorities are. Yes, we get stereotyped as pedants.

As I left the theater I heard people exclaiming to each other how irritating that would be, dealing with someone like Radcliffe. I felt like we had one chance to introduce ourselves to America and we had to start with our weirdest uncle. The guy who played the farting corpse in his last big movie.

(He's fabulous—no ironic wordplay intended—by the way. Cherry Jones and Bobby Cannavale too. Cannavale is delicious as the classically conceited writer, smirking Byronically in his pajamas.)

I got into fact-checking as a way to enter this world of people who care about and engage with words. As you say, I was surprised to find out that it was a way to engage with people who have nothing to do with this world. Because I'm a fact-checker I got to speak with a kid living in one of the world's largest refugee camps, and a man who's set the record for tying cherry stems with his tongue, and a young woman in New Orleans who was unbelievably upbeat for someone who had recently been strangled by her boyfriend. I've had to ask Greta Gerwig about the time she peed herself in seventh grade. I think the other day I heard you call someone back to verify details about their dog and we both looked at each other like, "What a weird job." I didn't expect any of this. I still don't.

Who are the people or the moments you can't forget? You've been at this longer than I have, I think. It's like we're supposed to be working these stories with gloves on, but they leave their marks. People stay with me, harrowing experiences stay with me. Political stories can mess me up for weeks. Subjects with totally reprehensible views get on the phone with us and speak reasonably with us, like human beings, and I don't always know if that's a triumph of civility or a failure. Are we not doing enough?

I notice tricky details in other stories too, and when I see language that looks extremely careful I wonder if I'm seeing thumbprints from a fellow checker. I wonder, too, about what tricky details mean to different writers.

Sometimes I think writers use impressive stats as a way to signal their own virtuosity (which is probably embarrassing for them when we have to re-report and fix those stats). Are those details supposed to be the brown M&Ms of the publishing world? The Van Halen story is connected in my mind with a Malcolm Gladwell or Gladwellesque story I remember reading about Honda. Apparently, they brought in a consultant to figure out how they could increase profit margins, and the consultant realized they were taking a lot of care with elements of the care people would never see. The moral of the story was, I think, that you have to impress people with what they can actually see, but I came away from it sad, thinking about all those Honda engineers reverently engaging with the seams inside the seams of the engine. As Gerwig puts it in *Lady Bird*, attention is love. Also a few weeks after I read the story, Honda had its faulty airbag crisis. So maybe those small unseen elements matter. Nice try, Gladwell!

There's so much I want to ask you, but on the subject of care: Do you think that fact-checking can be, in a weirdly Daoist way, counterproductive? Most people don't take advantage of us, but there are writers who skate by for years knowing that the checkers assigned to their piece will do the hard work. It's fun to imagine a world where there's a sort of ingredients list that comes with the article: 77% writer, 12% checker, 11% soybean oil. Or, for that matter, a world where checkers get bylines.

Looking forward to your thoughts!
Jamie

From: Alex Carp
Date: Mon, Oct 29, 2018 at 12:08 AM
To: Jamie Fisher
Subject: Re:

Hi Jamie,

To answer your question, I guess I felt the artificiality of the form was fitting because it reminded me of the tension that can come up between what it seems like fact-checkers are often thought of doing (establishing whether something is true or false, full stop) and what the job can actually feel like, which is giving over facts that will then be presented inside the inertia of a story, which can make an argument or portray a character in countless other minor, nuanced ways. There have definitely been articles that I know are accurate but that I think are wrong nonetheless—I do give my two cents on editorial decisions when it seems relevant, but accurate isn't always the same as true. And here we are, having an exchange that is true, but less than completely organic, and for a silent audience.

Your takeaways from fact-checking are really great. I've been able to speak with some really amazing people as well, but it's sometimes hard to feel connected with them. What I end up remembering more than I like are the mistakes and near-misses, or times I felt like I was really looking at the underbelly of a magazine or of the industry. For example, at a previous job, I heard a story about what was called "Rebecca's million-dollar mistake," that involved a story about some distressed part of the city that ran with photographs of the area. One of the story's photos showed a woman standing on the street, who was not part of the reporting and not named, but the photo caption said something about the prostitution in the neighborhood. It might have even said the photo depicted a prostitute. Either way, Rebecca, the checker, didn't ask about it, and the page went to press. The woman saw the photo and sued the magazine, and the lawsuit was prevented only when the magazine's lawyers found a newsstand that had sold that issue a day early (on a Sunday instead of a Monday), putting the lawsuit outside of the statute of limitations by one day. The whole thing feels a little gross, and it was a reminder that at a lot of places, fact-checking is simply there to help protect against lawsuits. Which is really not what I think either of us have in the front of our minds when we go about it from day to day.

I mean, I also made a friend who works in another part of the office because he walked by my desk and overheard me asking the celebrity subject of a profile about vaginal steaming, the kind of conversation I don't think twice about having in the fact-checking department, but I suddenly realized would be absolutely bizarre in almost any other line of work.

And then, of course, are the people who are so happy that their stories are going to be out in the world. One of my favorite calls recently was with a member of the San Francisco Symphony, checking a piece for a recent kids section. I could tell that this woman really just loved what she was doing, and she wanted the details about how an orchestra works to be right, but she also clearly took so much joy in talking about it. I love conversations like that.

Can fact-checking be counter-productive. In the long term, maybe? Probably? It definitely has its frustrations when it seems like we're doing someone else's work. I know what you mean about writers who can take advantage of checkers by knowing someone will be there to clean up their mess. And there are also the writers who fit into this category even though they might not realize it! So much of fact-checking can be balancing the needs (and egos) of people who aren't seeing eye to eye. What is your approach to those sorts of situations? Do you see it as just part of the job?

One of the other things I was curious about was how (or if) your work as a checker has changed your relationship to your own writing. I know that there are checkers who also do reporting, or write fiction, or play music, etc, and that there can be a reputation that fact-checkers who want to write would do so in an overly precise or pedantic way—though, of the checkers I know who write or writers who came from checking, that seems to hardly be the case. Has your job fact-checking stories changed the way you write, or even, have your writing inclinations changed the way you do your day job?

Talk to you soon,
Alex

From: Jamie Fisher
Date: Tue, Oct 30, 2018 at 7:29 PM
To: Alex Carp
Subject: Re:

Hi Alex,

Ohhhh the poor woman!! That's heartbreaking. It's just the kind of thing my paranoid former boss would have caught—he made me Nexis an editor's age. No unnamed people in pictures who were unnamed to us. I almost feel that photographic fact-checking is a different job, and sometimes I resent having to do it. Those captions that come in last-minute, promising to be fact-free and ultimately requiring a last-minute call to, say, the Afghan military.

That said, bouncing off the oft-promised fact-free caption or editorial addition: if you aren't trained as a fact-checker, it's hard to know what counts as a fact! I think people—even magazine people—tend to assume it's an outright definition or statement about the world, when it's probably something closer to an inherent proposition, explicit or implied, that makes a statement about the world. I remember being trained briefly almost as a bonus at my first internship. Just a workshop with bagels where one of the assistant editors explained how she had checked a recent complicated article. I looked at the first sentence and realized that I understood the concept of fact-checking but had no idea how it was done in practice. "What part of the sentence do you check?" I asked. She was baffled. "All of it," she said.

Neither one of us really understood what the other person was saying. I was trying to ask what in the sentence counted, according to our peculiar framework, as a "fact." And she did mean that all of the sentence was a potential fact, but that doesn't tell you how to break a sentence down and check it. As we both know from working on a certain philosopher's profile, there's something philosophical in the procedural elements of breaking the sentence down, a limited kind of philosophy that makes axioms but doesn't necessarily proceed to assemble greater truths.

If it's worth spelling out here: "The coat is red." Is it red and not reddish-orange? Does one person think it was red but not the other? Is it definitely a coat and not a sweatshirt? Should we be more precise and clarify that it's a very sweatshirt-like coat, or are we getting pedantic? Is it *the* coat or simply *a* coat because there are several coats in a pile?

And then of course if it's "The coat is red, she said"—what if she did really say that, word for word, but the coat isn't red or the red thing isn't a coat? A different way of saying, as you put it, that the facts are correct but the whole is wrong. Accurate but not true. What makes me most nervous is an authoritative-sounding speaker who ends up not being an authority.

Yes, egos are between sixty and ninety percent of the job, depending where you work. Ha! Here I think it matters much less, but you have to be so careful, and the editors carry the culture of where they started with them. A *GQ* editor is very different from an *Awl* editor. And depending on the editor you get, you get a different story.

Certain editors you know won't be interested in finessing out a small, particular detail (she said the coat was red, but it appears to have been reddish-brown) and so the whole back-and-forth gets cuts. Other editors would see the discrepancy as relevant information—if, say, we're not talking about coat gradients but a scholarly disagreement over economic principles. (And if the sentence is something like, “The coat was red with the blood of children, she alleges”—well, now you have to run a statement from the other party no matter what the editor thinks.)

Depending on the checker assigned to a particular story, and her willingness to push back, you’ll get a different piece. You’ll get, essentially, different facts.

I don’t know how to manage it, honestly. Sometimes I’m afraid to say what I think. I admire your ability to gently weigh in editorially at times. Being willing to say, for example, that we’ve left the voices of an affected population out of the piece—that takes bravery and it takes more work on your part.

Fact-checking affects my writing primarily in that it gives me something to do besides write! I think it’s good to be exposed to the world, to get out of your own head. I think I write as I normally would and then turn on my checking brain after the first few edits. Ex., when I first wrote the review of *The Lifespan of a Fact*, I misspelled the checker’s name and was sure the book had come out in 2015, when I was getting started as a checker. All that was fixed in a later round—and while we’re on the subject, isn’t it amazing how memory works? Memory constructs and daisy-chains what’s significant to us, not what “really” happened. It fits my story for *The Lifespan of a Fact* to mark, in some ways, my apprenticeship, and so, for at least a few years, it did.

How has checking affected your own writing, and your understanding of memory? Mostly I think we confirm what people remember, and most people only remember the events and people in the real world that intersect meaningfully with them. I’ve gotten to a point where I trust no one’s memory, especially my own (and that’s certainly affected my writing), but I still respect that their understanding of what happened is personally meaningful to them, even if it bears no relationship to the truth.

Talk soon,
Jamie

From: Jamie Fisher
Date: Tue, Oct 30, 2018 at 8:20 PM
To: Alex Carp
Subject: Re:

I mean, to dig into the title *The Lifespan of a Fact*: it implies that facts are mortal, and if we accept that this is true (I think it is, even if the play suggests they are because Facts are being valiantly sacrificed for Art or something), it is true because of memory.

I'm thinking about a recent book about survivors' narratives from the Armenian genocide. Towards the end these women were being paraded from commemorative event to commemorative event, asked to narrate stories they could no longer remember, with prodding from well-meaning facilitators, "And then they came in the hut, right, grandma?" "Yes yes, right."

There's a special poignancy here that comes from personal memories not inscribed in national histories; the survivors attest to the basic fact that the genocide happened (even if a testimony is not the kind of evidence that will satisfy the skeptical), but also that their private stories intersected with public history in a way that was meaningful. These facts have a very real lifespan.

I know you've explored oral histories recently, reading *These Truths*. But I'm wondering if you've thought about the frailty of memory and oral history as a broader principle, beyond what we would strictly consider oral histories. What we consider magazine journalism, perhaps.

I'm curious to hear what you think of all this! Waking up at midnight from my time away from work by ideas about my work, lol. And more seriously thinking about Pittsburgh.

Stay safe,
Jamie

From: Alex Carp
Date: On Sat, Jan 5, 2019 at 10:32 PM
To: Jamie Fisher
Subject: Re:

Hi Jamie,

After a bit of a break, here we are again. I've actually been spending a lot of the time since our last email looking into the history of fact-checking, for an essay that started out as something about the play *Lifespan of a Fact* but has morphed a bit into something like a cultural history of fact-checking. Did you know that the first two fact-checkers, both at *Time* magazine in the 1920s, quit their jobs, citing exhaustion? And after only a couple of months, I think. (Still trying to get to the bottom of that.) I also took a freelance job fact-checking a podcast, which has some unique challenges.

Also, looking over some of the questions we got in response to part of our conversation so far, I started to wonder about Quenton's question about what a fact is. Do you think various checkers have different answers for that? At first glance I took it as one of those questions that can make you a little dizzy, but once I tried to answer it, I realized that when I'm checking an article, I sort of break things up into the world constructed within the story itself, the thoughts or opinions of the writer / the world within the writer's head, and the outside world—if that makes any kind of sense—and that I think of facts as anything that reaches from one of those first two worlds into the third. (This makes it sound less like philosophy—what is a fact?—than a kind of translation.) And pretty soon after, I realized that is probably not how other fact-checkers do it?

But this system does relate to the other question, regarding the merits of fact-checking by phone or email, or actually, in person, out in the world. I can't say that I've never gone out in the world to check something, but it's been really rare. The only example I can think of is an essay about a sandwich shop I checked once, and the shop was actually in my neighborhood—the writer had left in a lot of physical description of the place itself, his sourcing was, let's say, less than ideal, and no one at the store would pick up the phone, so I just stopped by. (I also heard a story about a checker who was assigned a short profile of an up-and-coming television actress, who insisted the checker come by her apartment in Tribeca. It sounded like a very awkward scene.) Checking by phone and email, though, we do that all the time! (Quenton, you're part of the exchange now! Also, if it helps, email is used a lot when you need answers from an institution, especially an institution with a press office, or a person who is famous or powerful enough to become a kind of mini-institution themselves.)

I was also a bit intrigued by the question about how we check words and neologisms—especially after overhearing you at your desk this week, having to explain, I think, the difference between a creole and a dialect? What exactly were you diving into?

Looking forward to hearing your thoughts, as usual.
Alex

From: Jamie Fisher
Date: On Tue, Jan 8, 2019 at 3:29 PM
To: Alex Carp
Subject: Re:

Hi Alex,

I didn't realize the play had started an interest in our history! This is like how Roots sparked an interest in genealogy. (Or, on second thought, not at all.) It's interesting how specific histories are a gateway drug to Big Histories, or how fictional projections of history—a play, a novel—can renew our appreciation for the original object.

For my part, as I think I've mentioned before, the more I check the more interested I am in journalists who go unchecked (I guess in both senses of the word!) and are found out. Jayson Blair, Stephen Glass, Jonah Lehrer scenarios. I think a lot of white men who project self-confidence get away with more. And I think, generally speaking, that certain stories reaffirming popular or convenient narratives tend to escape notice. Did you hear about the reporter from *Der Spiegel* who made up a plausible but entirely incorrect story about a small town in Minnesota? Painting it as Trump country? Apparently he's done this for years. It's the kind of easy, blithely anti-American narrative that crowds out the more difficult American narratives. I just googled to look up the name—Claus Relotius—and, I swear to God, there was a write-up in the *Atlantic* along the same lines: "A motif of Relotius's work is America's supposed brutality. In one story, he told the macabre tale of a woman who travels across the country volunteering to witness executions. In another, he related the tragic experience of a Yemeni man wrongly imprisoned by the United States military at Guantánamo Bay, where he was held in solitary confinement and tortured for fourteen years.

(The song that American soldiers turned on full blast and pumped into the poor soul's cell? Bruce Springsteen's "Born in the U.S.A.") Both stories were complete fabrications. The conclusion is that Relotius told readers "what they wanted—what they expected—to hear about America."

Which moves to your taxonomy for facts, which I quite like. I have a similar division, which I think I picked up from my time in linguistics (she said gravely, as though it were a military tour): nesting is important. To circle back, it's not just "the coat was red" or "she said the coat was red," it's "what does it mean that the coat is red? Whose narrative does it serve?" In the piece I'm checking now, there are a few descriptions that are technically correct but that I feel are designed to produce a series of easy associations in the readers' mind, circumstantially supporting the idea that one of the protagonists is acting on nefarious principles. A fact can be true in a limited sense (all its words are true) and false in a broader sense (the universe it promotes is false). It's harder to argue with a writer about the latter.

I see physically visiting something to fact-check it as a literal manifestation of the job, as well as part of the job of journalism generally—to communicate immediacy and first-handedness. It's a jokey image, but I think of those weathermen who stand out in the hurricane in their yellow rain-jackets. They're totally unintelligible, but they're out by the pier at Vanderbilt Beach, attesting to the storm. We notarize an experience that someone else isn't participating in. I think this function will become more important as audio and video manipulation gets more sophisticated.

Along those lines, it occurs to me that the most successful non-fiction podcasts are those that, like Serial, tend to interrupt the narrative with themselves—with a "this part gets tricky," a "but let's back up a sec," a personal observation, an offhand gesture of authenticity. Theoretically that throws a scrim between the listener and the story, but in practice it ties them together. It destroys the idea of a story as pure, Platonic narrative that you passively observe and reduces it to a relationship between people. The listener, the reporter, the subjects.

On that note: hello, audience! Welcome to the story.

Best,
Jamie

* This text is a transcription of a workshop with Michael Portnoy. It was edited by the Department of Speculative Facts.

Michael Portnoy

Underbelly Business*

EXERCISE

Michael Portnoy: It's a lot of mingling that we're going to do. Does everyone have a pen and a piece of paper?

[PARTICIPANTS GETTING PENS AND PAPER]

Michael: What we are going to do first is use this text to mine notions that we will create, by recombining some words in the text itself. You can see them as a kind of jargon. And what we're trying to do is create two or three word phrases that are multipurpose, that can be used to describe phenomenon across many disciplines and are ambiguous enough so that they are provocative yet they don't really give away their meaning. What I also do sometimes is take words and add suffixes to them just to make them a bit more strange. So if you use the -ing suffix it makes them a little more concept-y. And you shouldn't think too hard on them, it's more like there needs to be a special buzz between the words and don't think too much about what the phrases mean, they just have to have a special radioactive connection between each other.

[PARTICIPANTS ARE WORKING]

Michael: Ok, let's share our terms and then we're gonna move on.

[A SAMPLE OF SOME OF THE NOTIONS CREATED BY THE PARTICIPANTS]

genocide valiance
byline skating
strict oral intersect
snackbar stereotyping
stage checking
brain gradients
language back camps
upbeat irritant

Michael: Now we're going to be playing a group of experts and to interrogate each other in front of the group. You'll take one of your concepts, and choose someone in the room, and then say, "X, I've heard you've developed the theory of the "upbeat irritant" for example, in the realm of…" and then insert a general topic here, so "in the realm of environmental science, or finance or, in relation to bioterrorism…" for example.

Participant: So I heard that "oral midnight Honda engineers" are doing the Tooth Fairy's dirty work now; maybe you can tell us more about that?

P: It's the growth of the population, and since this government enforced the law of the three-child minimum, we realized that cultural work relies a lot on the manufacturing of totem culture, and midnight stories, and therefore the tooth fairy, for example, is one very easy character, same as the hair frog, and together creating ideas such as fact-free captions to the children, and misspelled truths…

P: What is the idea of fact-free captions again?

P: It's more an existence that is freewheeling.

P: Is that even possible today though?

P: That's what we're trying to achieve through early education. We try to invest in the young and so, for example, finessing children's pajamas, was one way to bring it in.

P: The theory of finessing children pajamas?

P: In the comfortable growth. Because the theory was derived with pajamas, just like if you grow a pumpkin with a tight metal brace you can make very interesting shapes, and pajamas can conform a child's mind, so the theory is you can control the growth of a generation.

P: Just like how you would control the bookcases of dictionaries.

And J, your work, in cognitive linguistics is groundbreaking to say the least, we're paralyzed because of your theory of "statute prostitution" in the verb-noun relationships.

P: It's not an easy concept. So I'll try to keep it simple. I've tried to explain it to my cousin who lives in the countryside, so I also try to imagine someone who doesn't have a lot of experience in the field, and he loves fishing so he always goes there to fish by himself. So he's from a very different field, he's a very simple person and he's a worker and not an academic like us. So trying to understand this very complex system you need to basically find something in the realm of his field to make it understandable. So I also tell this theory of statute prostitution as something that relates to fishing; basically the moment that you throw out the line with the flesh that you've put on, to how it affects the whole lake. You don't think about it in the beginning...

Michael: But language has to think about it, doesn't it? It's hard for language to have a good night's sleep, as they say.

P: It's about prostitution of your mind.

Michael: And the lake in the realm of cognitive linguistics, what is that? La parole, or whatever they say?

P: That's the image that you project, it's not the reality so you're just projecting an image by throwing this flesh into the lake. But in the end it's more about the action of doing something in reality, the action that is a verb but at the same time the lake that is a noun.

P: I would like you, as a graphic designer, to talk about all the "relevant discrepancies" within the fonts that you have designed lately.

Michael: [INTERVENES] To me, "relevant discrepancies" in your question seems a bit too concrete and unambiguous, unless you're going to treat it like an abstract theory. You see what I mean? Let's just try to confuse it a bit.

P: I appreciate your question, and am happy to expand on this theory that, of course, you know was not developed by myself but I am a very big advocate of it, coming forth and thinking about where it comes from, the whole relationship between cognitive reading in a foreign place and the discrepancy between what you see and what you experience, to produce "desirable difficulty." Coming from that kind of detachment of reality and of reading language that I bring that to font making, and I'm really interested in making fonts that nobody can read. I really appreciate your attention towards the subject, which I think is very urgent in today's society where everybody reads too much.

Michael: Let's stand up and continue using your terminology. We've gotten to know each other a little bit, about our fields and theories and it would be great for us to also get to know some of your other theories so we're just going to converse with each other randomly. Maybe you've heard some ideas of some of the people here that relate to your work so just go up to the person that interests you and talk to them a bit and I'll also be handing you some further instructions, while you're talking. So when you get one of these cards just read it over and let that kind of further direct you within this room. But don't share them with anyone else.

P: The one-way thoughts don't reach any productivity, they keep on hitting the wall of my brain.

P: Maybe that has to do with your format-charisma? What do you think?

P: I don't believe in charisma, I think that is absolutely a strangled question. I believe in urban saults and mechanisms that are illogical because I think that's the only way to go further.

P: Further where?

P: Into the direction of the better.

P: The better… I think that's the problem with fact-checking: it comes down to good and bad facts, but it's such a faulty airbag. How much do we spend on fact-checking, they die while checking.

P: Why do they put so many experts in one room, what should they figure out? Maybe we should dance with each other?

P: It used to be called yellow journalism, when it couldn't be established as fact and yellow journalism comes actually from the color of the paper that they would print unverified stories on, in combination with the highlighter that they would use. It's actually really interesting when it comes to the history of journalism.

language
BACK CAMPS

Byline Skating

STATUTE

PROSTITUTION

BRAIN GRADIENTS

UNDERBELLY
BUSINESS

Director of Derailment All your ideas slip off the track on to another one that is obliquely related, or on to one that is completely unrelated. At times, there may be a vague connection between the ideas; at others, none will be apparent. Ex: "The next day when I'd be going out you know, I took control, like uh, I put bleach on my hair in California."

Director of Introductions You introduce people to people, sometimes physically bringing them together from across the room. You give lengthy invented introductions — "You must meet George! He is the only living authority on 16th C. Persian pistachio farming!"

Director of Interpersonal Shaping Your job is to go up to people who are talking to each other and re-position their bodies together so that the shapes they form are more peculiarly intimate, dynamic, twisted. Look at the pair and shape their bodies to bring out the things you think need to be brought out.

Director of Clanging Sounds rather than relationships of meaning govern your word choice. In addition to rhyming, your speech may also include punning associations, so that a word similar in sound brings in a new thought. Ex: "Many moldy mushrooms merge out of the mildewy mud on Mondays." "I heard the bell. Well, hell, then I fell."

Director of Faulty Conclusions Your conclusions are not reached logically. You make logical inferences between two clauses that are unwarranted or illogical. Or you make faulty inductive inferences.

Ex: "Do you think this will fit in the box?" draws a reply like "Well duh; it's brown, isn't it?"

Director of Stilted Speech Your speech is excessively formal. It may seem quaint or outdated, or may appear pompous, distant or over-polite.

Ex: "Whereas the attorney comported himself indecorously, the physician behaved as is customary for a born gentleman."

Director of Experimental Jokes You speak only in jokes which you make up on the spot. The jokes are more like strange tales and rarely have punchlines, and they end when you get bored. When someone is talking to you, you grab some words from their last sentence (ex: aqueducts) and say, "That reminds me of the one about the two (aqueducts) having sex in Venice. Etc."

Director of the Word Order, or Faulty Translation You like playing with the order of words like some people like playing with wood blocks. Before you speak each sentence, see each word as a block and do some rearranging. You speak as if you are doing so through a very bad translation program.

Director of Vocal Graphing As you speak, you are exceptionally aware of the pitch of each word and the shape your speech would draw on a graph. Your primary concern is that each of your sentences draws a pleasing shape of peaks, valleys, long slopes and curves. You let vocal melody drive your content, rather than the content itself.

Director of Terms Your primary concern is littering your speech with new terms, which you invent on the spot. Things like "Hormonal Loaning" or "Mental Stowaway," for example. You introduce these terms and then proceed to explain them in ways which don't necessarily need to make sense.

Director of Behavior You may change the behavior or speech of anyone in the room by going up to them and whispering a command into their ear.

For example: "I command you to: Start itching!," or "I command you to: Tell the person you're talking to that you want to chew on their eyeballs!"

Director of Closed-Eye Intrusive Dances Your only desire is to go up to people who are talking and dance very close to them with your eyes closed for a minute at least.

The tighter you shut your eyes, the better the dance will be.

Director of Advice Everything you say is in the form of advice. After every sentence your conversational partner says you have some advice to give. Or you can walk up to someone and offer it randomly.

For example: "In an age of agitation, keep your 'andante'! Say over and over to yourself: 'More, more andante,' trying to get where you need to be."

Director of Projects You use every interaction as an inspiration to conceive art projects, ideas for films, etc. So, someone is talking about their profound distaste for cucumbers and you say, "Picture this! It's a short film, shot through a thinly sliced cucumber, of a cucumber merchant coughing on his cucumbers, etc." And you develop this project during the conversation.

Director of Snooping You take someone in the room over to other people who are talking and you spy on their conversation and whisper commentary and counter-opinions to each other about it.

Director of Toasts In the middle of your conversations, you constantly make rambling, oblique toasts to completely tangential subjects.

Ex: [Ding ding ding] "Here's to the sultans of litigation! May they continue their brave mission to..."

Director of Innovations You see the next step in everything (mostly impractical). Whatever someone says, you mine it for things to riff off of, improve, permute, and combine with other things. Instead of carrying on a conversation, you just spit out idea after delirious idea based on the words you just heard.

Director of Epic Metaphors
Every sentence you say contains an absurdly overextended metaphor. Or metaphors nested within other metaphors. You launch into the metaphor having no idea where you are headed and continue and continue until each metaphor becomes a story in itself.

Director of Micro-Aerobics You are always leading low-volume micro-aerobics classes, trying to get people to move their body parts small distances (10 cm or less) in weird rhythmic patterns. You don't mind if anyone follows your counts. You are a good counter and have a huge smile.

Director of Misplaced Emotions
You are constantly experimenting with the amplitude and placement of emotions. You get angry, aroused or terrified, etc. at all the wrong times, in all the wrong quantities.

Director of Mysteries You see everything as if a crime has just occurred. You explain the situation, the evidence, etc. and ask people to solve it. Once you've presented the case, you can find new people and new mysteries. You also help people to behave more mysteriously.

Director of Things You control the placement of things and the way they move through the room. Without drawing too much attention, you are constantly reconfiguring objects (chairs, cups, shoes, etc.) to make arrangements that please you. You like to take certain objects on complex choreographic routes from one place to the next.

Director of Histories You are an authority on the (fictional) history of absolutely everything around you and talk about nothing else. You know lamps, rugs, noses, blouses and wall treatments, etc. and if you don't you better pretend you do. You are always looking around you (or within the sentences of your conversational partner) for things to share the outlandish histories of.

Director of Accelerated Interviews
You interview people, but jump right in there as if you'd already been talking to them for an hour. Your first question is always a follow-up (ex: "And how exactly did you domesticate the Philadelphian?"). And please don't worry about things like transitions or witty comments —question, question, question.

Department of Speculative Facts: The *New York Times*' new slogan says "Truth. It's more important now than ever." Do you find this slogan conservative, like in the face of online disinformation? Are things so bad that we should just be happy with the stable old truth of yesteryear?

Michael Portnoy: Well what's more urgent than facts themselves, is finding a way to make people believe in them again. I've been waiting to hear some solid ideas about how to restore people's trust in quality journalism.

DoSF: The far right seems to be successfully utilizing nonsense and baffle tactics—Pizzagate, memes or fake news—while progressive forces plod along at the pace of sensible logic and stable truth.

Michael: We should clarify what we mean when we talk about nonsense, as the word encompasses way too many different forms and approaches. There's a big difference between, say, Donald Barthelme, James Joyce or Conceptual Poetry, and Pizzagate. And a big difference between poetry and disinformation. With Pizzagate, the content is false but the structure of the information is conventional and simple. They're well-formed sentences that don't have a lot of ambiguities in them, where everything is fairly clear. Compared to poetry, most disinformation has very few degrees of ambiguity in it. Progressives, though, could certainly add some warped poetics to their toolbox, simply as a way to put a puzzling grappling hook into people's minds.

DoSF: Donald Trump is being called a Dadaist poet by some people.

Michael: An unintentional one, sure! After all the damage is done to the country, we at least can be thankful he gave us "covfefe." Did you ever see this attempt to diagram Trump's sentences?[1] It was a sprawling, branching drawing where they were trying to understand what is the subject, the object, and what is being modified, which is virtually impossible because he never really finishes a thought. His verbal output is a string of loosely connected sentence fragments.

1 http://www.slate.com/blogs/lexicon_valley/2015/07/31/donald_trump_this_run_on_sentence_from_a_speech_in_sun_city_south_carolina.html?via=gdpr-consent

DoSF: During the workshop we created neologistic phrases out of existing words; giving them content by making up and performing their meaning. Is it possible to know or feel if something is too random, or if it in fact is productively balancing between nonsense and sense?

Michael: Well of course this isn't a fine science, it's poetry, but I do think you're putting your finger on something important. Over the past years I've been looking into psychologists who study confusion and difficulty in learning and what amount of confusion, in art for example, arouses the curiosity. There's a threshold of tolerable confusion beyond which people lose interest. In the workshop we talked about the concept of "desirable difficulty," in relation to a new font that is very hard to read but makes people recall the information better because they're trying harder to understand the content. You shouldn't be able to get a clear idea initially of what the neologisms mean. I also like them to feel like a theory rather than a thing. Or if it is a thing it should be bound up with theory. I typically like gerunds, -ings, at the end of the phrase, like "perspective shunting," so it sounds like a process or phenomenon.

DoSF: In the workshop we took on different expertise roles, explaining our neologisms' relation to these fields. What to you is the relationship between ridiculizing and "expanding" expertise?

Michael: Rather than trying to ridiculize expertise, I was just borrowing the confidence of the expert and the formal qualities of expert-speak, as an engine for the participants, so they could better commit to the fleshing out of the strange notions they created.

DoSF: Can the workshop fail?

Michael: It can absolutely fail. In the workshop, I was already pointing to when the concepts can fail; anything too cutesy, silly or gibberishy isn't generative because it's too flat, too stable and doesn't arouse an aerial act of abstractions. Also, if there is a too one-to-one development of the concepts within the neologism, for instance when someone in the workshop gave a too logical and direct explanation of the words, instead of letting them sort of dance around each other and work upon each other. For instance, with "discourse slooping"—you can take "sloop" as a boat and just say it's a boat that people engage in discourse in, which would be too direct, rather than saying, "discourse slooping" is a theory from quantum linguistics which posits that every discourse is both leaning *into* a void and being leaned on *by* a void, and that void, if swaddled by its own projection *beyond* the gulch of consent, gobbles up enough content to fuel any form of verb-on-noun frottage, without that gummy aftertaste of shade neglect.

DoSF: Is it about letting go of control in that sense?

Michael: Yes, but you still have to have some appealing pattern and variations that happen within the unraveling of the concept. In all forms of improvisation, there is always some kind of formal system at work, you develop a pattern and vary it but you are also always fighting against expectations. By patterns here I mean, for example, the way you twist and develop and put variations on rhetoric devices—things from the outside which have recognizable syntactical structures which suggest sense. If you cede too much control and go for easy nonsense like "my pajama noodle got stuffed in the drain," it fails because it doesn't have theoretical implications.

DoSF: Do you also look for a balance between "the known" and "the unknown," by combining known words in unknown ways to create "new (un)knowns"? How do you balance this?

Michael: Well, a bunch of knowns such as images, associations and ideas should pop up when you hear the phrase, but since they never coalesce fully the phrase itself remains an unknown. Also, in the unspooling of the phrases, which we did in the guise of experts from various disciplines, the idea is to keep a nice balance between knowns and unknowns, concretes and abstractions. We didn't have time in the workshop for me to go into depth about the different ways to do this, but the unspooling should leave a lot of threads hanging and should convincingly weave together a tangle of ambiguities in appealing rhetorical patterns. I like to think the words have an electric charge between them, that they're like a radioactive compound. Part of this is the fecund irresolvability of the phrase, and the rest is a matter of sound, an alchemy of phonemes.

DoSF: So you are looking for a balance?

Michael: Yes, it's the type of ideas that that balancing act can generate. That type of world-building, the building of ontic spheres together, these compounds are interesting to me.

DoSF: What is the necessity of performance—would these neologisms also become "sensible" if the exercise/score was done through writing?

Michael: This kind of exercise works perfectly well in writing too, I've done these kind of exercises both in writing and performance. In performance there are all sorts of variables like character, mood, or pacing, tonality, that can add other nuances and layers to the meanings. In the end it's all about commitment to this nonsense, and to the train of the sentence and then veering it off track sometimes. When you are performing in front of your peers or an audience, there is a performance anxiety that can be more productive than when you are just alone with a piece of paper.
At the same time, there is also something to actually seeing the words on paper, in front of you, which makes you able to recombine them in a way that goes beyond the moment that they are used in a dialogue. They stay alive, and you have them in your hands to recombine in a more physical way than verbal conversations.

In some of my so-called *Relational Stalinist* performances, I find that the high-pressure atmosphere and the absurd dictatorial role I play helps spur people into playing with words and ideas more inventively. Because you almost have to be destabilized and pushed off the cliff in order to enter this more intuitive state of manipulating language or else you just get stuck in your habitual modes of creating meaning and sense and making yourself look clever.

DoSF: Do you find these strategies work as critique or satire?

Michael: I guess critique isn't my first thing. You can see it as some sort of critique or satire but I like to think of it more as a form of fiction-making—to see what other unusual ideas, forms and visions can be generated through the perverting of sense. But I see my work less as political or activist than as some sort of interpersonal program. A lot of what I do is trying to find new forms of togetherness which emphasize abstraction and alien logics.

DoSF: Edward de Bono, who is famous for his creative thinking books, defines a two-part creative process: Firstly, to break apart old logics and produce things that look like nonsense, then a second step to snap these broken logics back together into something that can be instrumentalized.

Michael: I'm not averse to that at all, and I think there's always something instrumentalizable within those broken logics. The word nonsense is a bit of a misnomer. Most rich forms of nonsense actually have a preponderance of meaning rather than none at all, which is why I prefer to call it "lutosense," from the Greek "luto," for mud, i.e. always slipping between sense and something less solid. I think that the truth in some forms of well-wrought nonsense is much more beneficial to the soul and intellect, as is, rather than anything that could potentially be boiled down from it.

Nicoline van Harskamp

Your Hearing has an Accent*

* This text has been compiled from transcribed workshop recordings and scripts for performance and video works by Nicoline van Harskamp. It was edited by Nicoline van Harskamp.

Nicoline van Harskamp: I read through the fact-checkers' letters and the first thing that struck me was that here are Alex and Jamie, guys with English-sounding names, sitting in an office in New York…

Participant: Jamie is a female Jamie.

Nicoline: Still, these people sit in an office of the *New York Times*, sending emails to each other. It's clear from the emails that they aren't just writing to each other, but are very aware of an audience of some kind.

P: Are they in the office? We didn't ask.

Nicoline: Fact is, that they are working for an English language news outlet in the U.S.. And I would like to propose we work on the relation between the English language and the world news, on the idea that "the truth speaks English."

Over the course of several projects I got to work with an actor and an actress with an interesting side job: they were pronunciation researchers for the audio version of a large English-language news magazine. That is an existing job in most global news outlets, from the BBC to Reuters, anywhere where they have to say the news out loud, basically.

Both of them are multi-multilingual. I would say they both do not have a defined native language. Generally, the terms "native language" or "native tongue" are very confusing and problematic and ideologically charged, but still, most people are quite happy to define what their native language might be. But these two were not. That makes them extremely flexible with spoken word and they work in different languages as actors.

P: Is anyone here like that?

P: No

Nicoline: I interviewed one of them last year for my work *My Name is Language*.

From: Nicoline van Harskamp, *My Name is Language / Mein Name is Sprache* (Scriptings; Archive Books, 2018)

My job is to scan every article for words that may be difficult to pronounce.
I sit there hooked on a computer.
Headphones in.

I do the ones that I know first.

Most of them are names.

For example, a new spider was discovered recently and its name had about fourteen syllables.

It's not ever meant to be said out loud, I think.

But I needed to go online and look up every potential video item where somebody actually says that name out loud.

The general job requirement is really to know as many languages as possible.

Because the more you know, the less you have to guess.

In theory, that is.

Because for example, there is…

So I underline in an article the name Mohammed.

I speak Arabic so I would say it's pronounced as /mə'xamd/

But it's about DJ Mohamed and he doesn't call himself /mə'xamd/.

So you can't just rely on how it should be said.

It's how the person himself says it or how most other people say it.

Anyway, when I've made a decision, I write down for the voice-over artist how something should be said.

There is no fixed system for that.

I tend to do it using capital letters for stresses and I say it out loud to them if I have to.

But there is no guarantee they get it right because by the time they get back to the recording booth, their mouth wants to say it again in another way.

And once they said it in one way, then the editors want to stick with the version of the name.

The most experienced voice artists also work for the BBC or Reuters, or whatever.

And a lot of the times they have already said the difficult names first, because the same names appear in the news cycles.

It's almost like: whoever pronounced it first… gets to decide.

Nicoline: I'd like to work together with you on phonetically checking the news of today. So, on the table there are two copies of today's *New York Times*, the international edition. I would like us to mark all names of places and people and find ways to pronounce them. We will have to go online, listen to YouTube videos in languages we might not understand, call people up on the other side of the globe, call up embassies and consulates and so on.

P: Is "Mississippi," for example, something that we would need to research?

Nicoline: It's up to you. I think most people say it the same way. But the question is: Who are we doing it for? If we are doing it for the *New York Times* and the fact-checkers are native speakers of American English, that's our target language. But the question then is: Who is the *New York Times* written for?

P: There is an emphasis problem. An Indian and a French speaker would put the emphasis in different places in the word Mississippi.

Nicoline: Exactly. We have to define for ourselves what it means to get the names "right." Is it how they would be pronounced by a "native speaker" of the language they are in? Are names part of specific languages, or do they occupy a different type of linguistic area? We could find out from which language the word Mississippi stems, and how it must be pronounced. But again, as in the example of DJ Mohamed, it's not only about getting it "right." And then, American names generally are so mixed, they are taken from different languages and then Anglified to a certain extend. In the United States, the public pronunciation of names is politically charged. For example, news anchors pronounce the name of Sonia Sotomayor, Associate Justice of the US Supreme Court, both with a "Spanish" mouth and with an "English" mouth. What does it mean to do either, from a political perspective? Is it empowering to use a Spanish pronunciation, or does it prescribe an "otherness" from the channel's core audience?

P: For example, with Qatar; do you say it the way the people who live in the place would say it?

Nicoline: Again, the question is what choice is made. The spelling of Arabic personal and place names in Roman alphabet, like Qatar, tends to be done through the phonetic properties of French or English, for reasons dating back to colonial times. And the spelling defines the pronunciation. So the question is, do we go to, say, the website of Qatar Airlines and check how the word is said there? Or do we find out how people in Qatar pronounce Qatar?

P: How do we write the difference down?

Nicoline: I work with International Phonetic Alphabet or IPA. It's a way of notating the spoken word through the anatomy of the mouth and the throat and the nose.

It is a system that precedes audio recording. You can still see it in most dictionaries, behind the spelling of a word. IPA uses a single symbol for a single sound, and so the idea of "spelling" is obsolete.

From: Nicoline van Harskamp, Englishes Mooc (2019)

Let's take a closer look at the consonants in the International Phonetic Alphabet.

A consonant is made when two parts of your mouth create an obstruction for your breath on its way out.

One part is active and one is passive.

The places of air obstruction here have names.

*BILABIAL: The upper lip is passive, the lower lip is active /***b***/.*

*LABIODENTAL: The upper teeth are passive, the lower lip is active /***f***/.*

*ALVEOLAR: Deals with a little ridge just behind your front teeth. When this alveolar ridge is passive and the tip of your tongue touches it, you can make a sound like /***d***/ or /***t***/.*

POST-ALVEOLAR: The passive bit is just behind the alveolar ridge, your tongue tip is active /ʃ/.

*PALATAL: Your soft palate is passive and the middle of your tongue is active /***j***/.*

*VELAR: The back of your soft palate is passive. The middle of your tongue is active /***k***/.*

*UVULAR: The little thing in the back of your throat is passive. The back of your tongue is active /***x***/.*

We need to consider not only the place of obstruction but also the manner.

*PLOSIVE: Air escapes in little puffs /***p***/.*

*FRICATIVE: Air escapes through a small opening /***s***/.*

*APPROXIMANT: Air escapes through a slightly bigger opening /***g***/.*

*TRILL: The active and the passive part of your mouth trill together /***B***/.*

*TAP OR FLAP: The active and the passive places touch briefly, just once /***ɾ***/.*

The IPA consonant chart identifies a vowel by combining a place and a manner of obstruction.

An alveolar approximant sounds like /ɹ/.

A uvular approximant sounds like /ʁ/.

*An alveolar trill sounds like /***r***/.*

An alveolar tap sounds like /ɾ/.

The orthographic transcription of these four vowels is usually an R. Languages that have been canonized to serve as so-called national languages, still have regional and social varieties when spoken. The pronunciation of R is a marker of difference in many languages, including all types of spoken English. In rhotic Englishes, every R is pronounced. So a word like "writer" can sound like

/ɹaɪtəɹ/ /raɪtər/ /ʁaɪtəʁ/

and so on. In non-rhotic Englishes, the R is not pronounced after a vowel at the end of a word, resulting in

/ɹaɪtə/ /raɪda/

Nicoline: You can also approximate the pronunciation using spelling from other languages. The pronunciation of a name like Feinstein can, in the American context, be written down as Feinsteen or Feinstayn, for example. But this can be very confusing because English spelling is irregular. And then there are certain sounds that are difficult to produce, or impossible to produce because not everybody is able to hear or reproduce everything. So, are you going to try to come closer to the "real" pronunciation or skip the sounds altogether? And what are your strategies for approximating or skipping certain sounds?

P: People do use different spellings in English when their language doesn't have the same alphabet, like Indian names for example.

Nicoline: Exactly. Here we have the name Modi in the paper. This name is a bit like Putin or Obama—names that have gotten such a prominent place in the news that they have become words in themselves. These names have become brand words. So Modi is kind of easy. But then we have Modi's first name, Narendra. Now the R is a big issue. In many languages the different pronunciations of R indicate a class or regional difference. By using an American R, the alveolar approximant, in Narendra, it's clear that we've Anglified the name.

P: I think people's names should be said the way they say it themselves.

P: Sometimes if you are not able to pronounce a name right, it feels more honest to almost translate it and Anglify it, so that it is at least transparent that you are making your own, English, version of it.

P: Is it a responsibility to learn these sounds? Like the very throaty R, the uvular approximant. If I would say it, it would almost seem as if I was faking an accent in a very weird way.

Nicoline: Yes, it could be a co-optation also, to mimic a pronunciation. It could sound like you make fun of someone's language.

P: Before I studied in India, I had a more North American accent that I got from living in Canada. But when I was in India, people didn't understand that accent very well. So I tried to speak more with a Norwegian accent and after a while my English became even more Hindi. I was trying to adjust to be understood, and Hindified the European words or names.

P: Instead of talking "as good as possible English," you actually changed it.

Nicoline: That is the big question: "What is as good as possible?" Indian English is also an official language, it's some people's "native language." So what variety of a language do you want to adapt to if you are not a native speaker of that language? In your case, being in India, that would have been indeed an Indian English.

But then, I prefer to use the word production instead of accent. Because accent implies some type of group variety of a language, such as a national accent. But people have their versions of languages, with traces of all sorts of places and experiences. The English that I speak is mine. It's colored by my own "linguistic biography." And I produce it in my own way.

Actually, there have never been so many people using the same link-language, English, ever before. Thinking of the number of people who are able to communicate in English, you would expect to have much more varieties than we actually do. But we tend to listen to the "center" of the language, to what we perceive to be "native" forms, like British or North American forms. We use "native speakers" to proof-read our English texts or record our voice-overs. If we would stop doing this, we would get a language that really represents the struggle with the different languages.

P: Why are not all names written in pronunciation language?

Nicoline: In IPA you would have the same problem because you would still standardize things. Not everyone pronounces things the same way. One of the inventors of IPA was later the model for Bernard Shaw's play *Pygmalion*, better known later as the musical *My Fair Lady*, in which the girl Liza Doolittle learns how to speak English "like a lady" from the Language Professor Higgins. He has developed a system of pronunciation and uses that to classify the speech of Liza against that of Higgins' friend, a colonel based in the then colonized India. The phonetic system is from the 1910s and fits the enthusiasm for classification, systematization, alphabetization of the things that were perceived to be yet unknown otherwise.

So today, we could categorize language names, we could try to standardize the pronunciation of names, but that attempt is built on the wrong premise. Things are always way more complex.

For example, here is an image from a performance script for *Some Name Some Noun Simply*. It was a piece where the actors needed to learn very distorted versions of language. On this page, you can see how the text lines are numbered, and there are IPA symbols underneath to indicate the intended pronunciation of a sentence. And then underneath that, the actor wrote in German how he understands the meaning of that sentence. I initially thought people could learn from the audio first, and I sent MP3 files with my own pronunciation of the sentences, along with the written script. But I soon realized that they couldn't learn the lines unless they would really understand what they were saying. And because there was no "competent" English original for this text, they had to figure out through our discussions, what the sentences mean. And then this actor was using German to remember the meaning, and Hindi to remember the pronunciation. So on this script page you find four languages in three different alphabets.

P: If you would transcribe in Phonetic Alphabet, then do you represent different voices, or do you do it in a prescriptive way, like it's done in the dictionary?

P: You can do both!

From: *Englishes Mooc*, Nicoline van Harskamp, 2019

The IPA in a dictionary shows you how something should be pronounced by a national or academic standard. It is a phonemic transcription of a word. An IPA notation of detailed, individualized features of one person's speech is called a phonetic transcription. It describes what is there, it doesn't prescribe what should be there, resulting in something as subjective and personal as a drawing.

There is no such thing as neutral hearing. Our own language background has as much influence on our hearing as on our speaking. Our hearing has an "accent." My phonemic transcription of your speech can tell not only how you have said something to me, but also how I have heard you. Phoneticians have to take so-called ear training as part of their education. An interesting way to do your own ear training, is by concentrating on people's names.

In a situation like the events today, very complex ideas are conveyed in vehicular languages. The words that usually remain untranslated, are names. Yet personal names are words that exist in particular languages. Your name is language. When somebody calls your name, you probably respond not to its meaning, but to its sound. Speaking a name from an orthographic transcription in, say, the Roman alphabet, is notoriously problematic. But even when you say your own name out loud as part of an introduction, people may not be able to repeat it, because they are unable to reproduce your sounds, or even to capture them with their ears.

So today, when somebody tells you their name, take a moment to write it down as you hear it from their mouth. If you are already familiar with IPA, make a phonetic transcription. If you aren't, write it in any other way that helps you to remember the sounds. You may discover sounds that you are not able to hear.

Nicoline: Okay, so let's try to let some of these *New York Times* articles be read up by one of the "native speakers" of English in the room.

In the UK, newsreaders still adopt British Received Pronunciation or RP. It is actually a regional accent of the South of English. Most people do not speak that way but use it to bring authority to their voice. It's what we learned in school in the Netherlands as the right way.

P: When we were kids learning English we just had to choose which celebrity we wanted to sound like.

Nicoline: "Newsreader," do you want to have a go?

P: *Hashtags for Pakistan and India. By Fatima Bhutto. Pakistan and India, two nuclear-armed states have fought many wars since partition in 1947. Our militaries have faced off in 1947, 1965, 1971 and 1999. Between those wars there have been numerous skirmishes cross-border strikes and accusations of covert support for terrorism. I have never seen my country at peace with its neighbor, no, neighbor but never before have I seen a war played out between two nuclear-armed states with Twitter accounts. On February 14th a suicide bomber hit a convoy of paramilitary forces in the Indian-controlled Kashmir.*

P: I have a friend from Pakistan and if I said */paki stan/* she would be like…

P: Totally.

P: I wouldn't put an */i/* there because then there would be */paki stan/* instead of */pakə stan/.*

P: */pak i/.*

P: Is that an American thing?

P: Well, I saw this in a Youtube video called "Obama's Most Un-American Pronunciations." People were criticizing him, like: "What is this exotic pronunciation?" Because he said */pakə stan/.*

P: Instead of what?

P: Instead of */paki stan/.*

Nicoline: There is something really weird with names because they are often not seen as part of a language. They are left untranslated and we find that completely acceptable—until we have to pronounce them. So, in that sense, names mark the fact that we are not speaking the same language, even if it seems that we are.

* This text is a transcription of a workshop with Mette Edvardsen. It was edited by the Department of Speculative Facts.

Mette Edvardsen

Departing from the Idea That Everything Exists Already*

Word count of e-mail:
From: Jamie Fisher
Date: On Tue, Jan 8, 2019 at 3:29 PM
To: Alex Carp
Subject: Re

42 the
26 a
19 in
19 I
17 to
16 it
15 of
14 that
12 's
10 and
8 as
7 is
7 are
6 think
6 more
6 but
5 who
5 up
5 story
5 for
4 with
4 was

Mette Edvardsen: The letter exchange between Alex and Jamie was an interesting entry into thinking about fact-checkers. At first, I didn't know how to approach your research. When I work I don't start from a topic. So I tried to connect the concept of speculative facts to my own practice in the way I do things and work with material. I first had the idea of relating facts to memory, as a process. I have worked with memory and the process of learning by heart. Memory is deceptive, it changes over time, and this raises questions about its source. In relation to facts and fact-checkers, I thought the practice of memory could be a lens to look through. But a workshop of this type would, obviously, need more than one day.

4 this
4 they
4 out
4 or
4 on
4 narrative
4 he
4 an
4 about
3 which
3 what
3 those
3 Relotius
3 red
3 part
3 like
3 how
3 coat
3 at
3 American
2 you
2 years
2 were
2 true
2 told
2 there
2 tend
2 't
2 stories
2 she
2 sense
2 said
2 reporter
2 readers
2 're
2 play
2 our
2 one
2 not
2 narratives
2 my
2 military
2 listener
2 lines
2 just
2 job
2 interest
2 important
2 idea

For our workshop, I used software to order the words from the fact-checkers' letters alphabetically. So we have the whole text in raw form as loose material. All the words are there, and in relation to the idea of fact-checking being so precise with language, there is an interesting question that the text touches upon: what is a fact and what is a word? Meanings of course change because of context. With all the words on the table, we will rewrite the text—all the words will be used in order to stay "true" to the original word count. We'll need to work fast, forcing us to find strategies together.

Participant: If you go looking for a specific word in the list, aren't you then just writing?

Mette: At first it's hard to go beyond meaning. We're quick to find and create meanings. But maybe if we dig in the material, after a while, we start to function in other ways, with other sensitivities, using other strategies, composing differently. It's not about avoiding meaning, but maybe changing our relation to it, or how we follow it. And the less words we have left to choose from, the more other ways we will need to find, such as working with a lot of the the the the's and words out of context. Chance will be imposed on us. But our resistance here is also productive. To refuse something can bring something else up. Usually, I need to figure out how to generate material, and the writing comes with that. But now we need another approach, of how to accept the material and work from there.

P: How does this working with text relate to bodies?

Mette: It's about how we are doing it. I think writing can be a very bodily practice or experience. Not in the sense that we sit in very weird positions when writing, but there are other tensions and involvements of the body. Being still, or sitting, doesn't make it less about being in the body. You're moving less when you are reading a book in your sofa than when you are walking in the woods, but you are not less in your body. And thinking is also doing. What is the relation between the body and reading, what is the space of reading, where does it take place?

P: Can you say a bit about how you problematize the reduction of language by instrumental reason, and link it to why you propose the exercise of today?

Mette: I work with imagination and how to activate that. It's about activating our capacities for thinking, projecting, imagining—seeing images, feeling, listening. All the things that make us up as humans who be, feel, know, act in the world. And language is a great device to work with for that, and as material very interesting. It's a poetic practice.

I come from dance and choreography, and language and speech was not so present for me in my work for a long time. But I have been working a lot with language in the past years. My interest is not in language as such. Language is there as a consequence of something else. I had worked a lot with objects and I became interested in the question:

2	history
2	histories
2	hear
2	gets
2	generally
2	from
2	false
2	fact
2	experience
2	easy
2	does
2	country
2	check
2	can
2	by
2	both
2	between
2	back
2	America
2	along
2	all
1	your
1	Yemeni
1	yellow
1	wrongly
1	writer
1	write
1	work
1	words
1	word
1	woman
1	witness
1	will
1	whose
1	white
1	where
1	well
1	welcome
1	weathermen
1	we
1	wanted
1	volunteering
1	visiting
1	video
1	've
1	Vanderbilt
1	universe
1	United
1	unintelligible

1 unchecked
1 U.S.A.
1 turned
1 Trump
1 tricky
1 travels
1 tragic
1 town
1 tour
1 totally
1 tortured
1 together
1 time
1 ties
1 throws
1 thought
1 though
1 theoretically
1 themselves
1 them
1 their
1 technically
1 taxonomy
1 tale
1 swear
1 supposed
1 supporting
1 successful
1 subjects
1 storm
1 Stephen
1 states
1 started
1 stand
1 Springsteen
1 Spiegel
1 specific
1 speaking
1 sparked
1 soul
1 sophisticated
1 song
1 something
1 someone
1 solitary
1 soldiers
1 small
1 similar
1 serve

What would I do if there would be no objects—if there would be nothing—to start from nothing? And with the disappearance of objects language came in.

For me performance is not primarily a visual art form, other senses are being engaged. My pieces are not visual. I often start in an empty space with nothing. Of course, there is something to see, but it's not driven by visual input. Language and speech gives other material to build with and opens up another access to what is there.

So what I thought we could do today is to (re) write the conversation between the fact-checkers together. To enter a process and discuss questions as they come up. How are we dealing with the material, the words on the table, and what decisions do we take along the way? Everything exists already, nothing can be added and nothing can be lost.

P: How does writing bring things into being?

Mette: In the piece *Black* (2011) the writing brings things into being in a quite direct way, to begin with at least. I name something and it exists. The interest was not in the first place about meaning, but more in looking at language as material and what it can do. I used language to create a world. I started with a physical limit, not a specific topic, which of course doesn't mean that there's no meaning. It's not about creating non-sense, but the sense of language as material, as written, as textures, as capacity—to open up the spaces of imagination. I use specific features offered by language (to name, to affirm), and I work with this in space (on stage) and in the relation between stage and audience. "Text" for me is a wider notion; it's both what is spoken/written, and also what is taking place in space. When I use text in my performances there is no hierarchy between the two. I don't write the text first and then stage the performance. It's taking place at the same time. For me all the elements are part of the writing, like movements in space, actions, and time. I consider all of this as "text," and as "writing."

P: Your project *No Title* (2014) looks into "what is not"—how does negating something produce something new?

Mette: Negation was opening up to everything else, to what is not. This was the piece I made after *Black* where I was naming and affirming things. In *No Title* I used negations and I was removing things by saying that they are "gone." Emptying out the space, and making everything disappear. There was a new movement. Instead of making things appear, I was now taking them away. It was interesting how this would work in the imagination, how images were created, and what happened to them. It's not enough to say that something is gone in order to take it away. And some things we can more easily take away (gone!) in our imagination than others. There is a paradox in the negation, because in order to say that something is "gone," first I have to name it to bring it there. So it was working with another elasticity of language.

1 series
1 serial
1 senses
1 self
1 see
1 second
1 sec
1 scrim
1 scenarios
1 same
1 roots
1 renew
1 relationship
1 related
1 reduces
1 realize
1 reaffirming
1 rain
1 quite
1 pure
1 pumped
1 protagonists
1 promotes
1 projections
1 project
1 produce
1 principles
1 practice
1 popular
1 poor
1 podcasts
1 plausible
1 platonic
1 pier
1 piece
1 picked
1 physically
1 personal
1 people
1 passively
1 participating
1 painting
1 original
1 offhand
1 occurs
1 observe
1 observation
1 object
1 now

1 novel
1 notice
1 note
1 notarize
1 non
1 nesting
1 nefarious
1 name
1 moves
1 motif
1 most
1 Minnesota
1 mind
1 mentioned
1 men
1 mean
1 me
1 manipulation
1 manifestation
1 man
1 made
1 macabre
1 m
1 lot
1 look
1 literal
1 linguistics
1 limited
1 let
1 Lehrer
1 latter
1 kind
1 journalists
1 journalism
1 Jonah
1 jokey
1 Jayson
1 Jamie
1 jackets
1 its
1 isn
1 into
1 interrupt
1 interesting
1 interested
1 incorrect
1 imprisoned
1 immediacy
1 image

Then also double negation, and triple—is that then more "not" than the "not not"? Or do they, the "nots," cancel each other out?

P: Could you explain your project *Time has fallen asleep in the afternoon sunshine* (2010–ongoing)?

Mette: In *Time has fallen asleep…* we are learning books by heart, quite literally, word by word. For me this is about literature, reading, the spaces of reading, the process—and capacity—of memory and how that works. The intention or starting point is clear, to learn a book by heart. Then once you begin, there's the choice of book, the memory practice, and the readings—a whole process—and it continues to grow and change over time. And we are at the same time witnesses to the process as well as inside of it, doing it, being it. It's not about true or not true. We are working with memory and time, stretching time.

P: How do you relate to facts in your work? How would you define a fact?

Mette: I don't relate to facts in my work. I make performances. It's fiction. It's constructed and subjective. A fact is the opposite.

P: Do you see a responsibility even within artistic practices to revalue the fact when it's losing ground within the world?

Mette: No, I don't think that's the responsibility of art. It can very well be that an artist chooses to work with that, and that would be totally fine of course. But art cannot be good or not good in relation to criteria. Art is not true or false. I think we need to be wary of instrumental doubt and fake balance, and inserting the quest for facts where it doesn't belong. But it depends on how you see art. Do you see it as communication, or do you think of it as an experience that is opening something, the unknown, a feeling? Or maybe just to bring us closer to ourselves, it doesn't always have to be about going somewhere else. Of course, what is going on around us in the world is part of who we are, how we are, and also the art we make. But I still think that we have to let art be art, and allow fiction to have its place. So, for our exercise, in our attempt at rewriting, how do we go beyond meaning but still in the sense that it's not just whatever? It means to build something in another way.

P: It does seem none of the texts we produced today are true. No one is writing something that they would argue as being true.

P: I would defend the sentence "painting is not non-fiction."

1 hurricane
1 hi
1 hello
1 held
1 have
1 harder
1 handedness
1 had
1 guess
1 Guantánamo
1 gravely
1 googled
1 god
1 go
1 glass
1 get
1 gesture
1 genealogy
1 gateway
1 function
1 full
1 fourteen
1 found
1 first
1 fictional
1 fiction
1 few
1 feel
1 facts
1 fabrications
1 expected
1 executions
1 escape
1 entirely
1 else
1 drug
1 done
1 division
1 difficult
1 didn
1 did
1 destroys
1 designed
1 descriptions
1 Der
1 crowds
1 correct
1 convenient
1 confinement

1 confidence
1 conclusion
1 complete
1 communicate
1 Claus
1 circumstantially
1 circle
1 checking
1 certain
1 cell
1 brutality
1 Bruce
1 broader
1 born
1 blithely
1 blast
1 Blair
1 big
1 best
1 before
1 become
1 beach
1 be
1 bay
1 away
1 authenticity
1 audio
1 audience
1 attesting
1 Atlantic
1 associations
1 argue
1 appreciation
1 apparently
1 anti
1 another
1 am
1 Alex
1 acting
1 across

* This text is a transcription of a workshop with an introduction written afterward by Kate Briggs. It was edited by the Department of Speculative Facts.

Kate Briggs

Reading is a Throwing Forward*

INTRODUCTION

Before we get to the exercise, I will tell you a bit about how I got interested in these questions by speaking about a project I did, called *Story the Story in It*. This was a collaboration with a psychologist called Sam Hutton, and involved eye-tracking my reading of a short story by Henry James called *The Story in It*. The first paragraph of this story reads like this:

The weather had turned so much worse that the rest of the day was certainly lost. The wind had risen and the storm gathered force; they gave from time to time a thump at the firm windows and dashed even against those protected by the verandah their vicious splotches of rain. Beyond the lawn, already vivid with the touch of May, showed a violence of watered green; the budding shrubs and trees repeated the note as they tossed their thick masses, and the cold, troubled light, filling the pretty drawing-room, marked the spring afternoon as sufficiently young.

EXCERPT 1

Recently, I published an essay in the form of a small book, called *Entertaining Ideas* (2019). I was—and, in many ways, I still am—happy with it. I gave copies to some of my friends, my colleagues. I was invited to read aloud from it at an event in London. And while I was preparing for the reading I noticed one, two, three, then four typos in the published book. I experienced that familiar sinking feeling of cheeks-stomach-hands turning hot then cold. These mistakes—of the order of missing words, homonyms of what should have been the right words, repetitions of the right words—all occurred within two pages of each other.

Sigmund Freud was famously interested in these kinds of minor mistakes: how commonly they occur, how they matter, what they reveal about the other mental processes at work. Unconscious processes that are actively and purposively altering the shared and apparently stable materials of the world. In *The Psychopathology of Everyday Life* (1901; the English translation by A.A. Brill appeared in 1914) there is a whole chapter on misreadings: anecdotal misreadings of signage, newspaper headlines, official as well as private letters. Freud writes:

> *In a very large number of cases, it is the reader's preparedness that alters the text and reads into it something which he is expecting or with which he is occupied. The only contribution towards a misreading which the text itself need make is that of affording some sort of resemblance in the verbal image, which the reader can alter in the sense he requires.*

The reader alters the text in the sense she requires.

In Freud's account these small mistakes always make sense. Some familiar or expected strange sense—oddly familiar at least to the reader, even if she has unconsciously, and only virtually, privately, altered a sentence to make it say something different, or new.

My typos were markers of the gap between what was printed on the page and what I thought I had received, which was also what I had wanted to receive (a clean text, ready to print, requiring no further work). Or, to put it another way: they were reminders that between the page-world and this particular brain receiving and seeking information from that page-world there is a process of mediation called reading.

I have a hard time reading Henry James. His sentences demand a certain amount of attention to figure out what's going on, but other than that I couldn't really get my head around why I found him so difficult to read. Then I came across the existence of a specific type of sentence called a "garden path" sentence which helped me to begin to explain it. I'll read to you know about what I once wrote about these:

Garden path sentences are sentences that are grammatically correct but misleading. The first part of such a sentence sets up the route ahead, allowing us to start building what linguists call a structure of meaning. But then we encounter a word or phrase that seems suddenly inconsistent with the structure we are in the process of building. Garden path sentences produce a brief moment of bewilderment in the reader: they interrupt or fork our path through a sentence, forcing us to go back to the beginning and work our way through it again, revising our structure, only this time with the fork in the path up ahead in mind.

"The old man the boat"

With "the old man," the sense of the sentence is being directed in one way. With "the boat," our progress is abruptly stalled. But interestingly, and the reason I haven't read the sentence out loud yet, is the ambiguity disappears when I do. When I read it out loud, my intonation makes it clear that "man" has to be the verb, the old operate the boat.

Thinking about these garden path sentences helped me to get a grip on why reading Henry James is difficult for me. I'm reading him, and at the same time I'm constantly aware of the attention I need to give to the process of reading, going back to the beginning of a sentence or a section of sentences and beginning again in order to proceed to the next. Reading Henry James, I become aware of the *action* of reading. The desire to make this action visible to myself is what prompted me to get in touch with a psychologist who knows a lot more about this than I do. Sam is a professor at the University of Sussex who works with eye-tracking and who I asked to help me make a record of my reading. I went to his lab in Sussex and took with me something that I knew I'd find difficult but that I had never read before. It mattered to me that the record was of a first-time reading. I took Henry James' *The Story in It* because I liked the title. It took me seventeen minutes and fifty-four seconds to read its twenty-one pages.

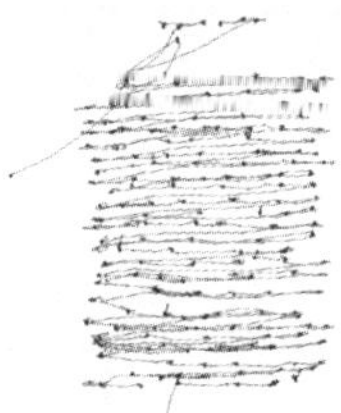

FIGURE 1

We made this image (Figure 1.) and as you can see the line my eye is making here is very dense; I am really concentrating. I had never met Sam before, so when I turned up at his office, sat down for a coffee and then all of a sudden started to read the

Mediation—is that the right word?
The only word?
Perhaps another is distortion.
Or transformation.
Or, as Freud sometimes puts it, translation.
To this short list, I would also want to add:
guess-work.

Published in the same decade as Freud's study, Edmund Burke Huey's *The Psychology and Pedagogy of Reading* (1908) uncovers what we are actually doing when we read. How fast the eyes move. Their back-and-forth skipping movements over the page. The frequency of their sudden leaps, or saccades, from one point of rest to another. He describes the series of tests he carried out to demonstrate how *very little* we actually "see" when we read:

> *In experiments made some years ago I found that [...] the upper half of a word or letter is obviously more important for perception than is the lower half [...], indeed we habitually find most meanings in the upper parts of objects; we are ourselves so placed and so orientated to bring this about.*

Huey illustrates this by way of an altered version of a well-known story.

And indeed look: it is still possible to read the first paragraph, with only the lower halves of the words removed, but very difficult to read the second.

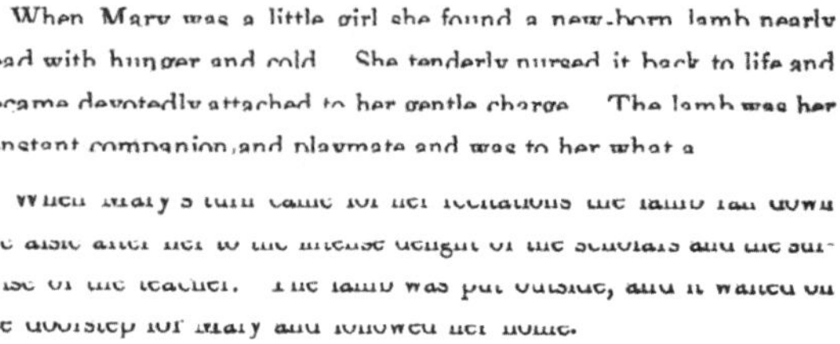

When Mary was a little girl she found a new-born lamb nearly dead with hunger and cold. She tenderly nursed it back to life and became devotedly attached to her gentle charge. The lamb was her constant companion, and playmate and was to her what a

When Mary's turn came for her recitations the lamb ran down the aisle after her to the intense delight of the scholars and the surprise of the teacher. The lamb was put outside, and it waited on the doorstep for Mary and followed her home.

Huey also discovered that "the first half of a word is of considerably greater importance for perception than is the latter half."

When reading, we are led by first parts and the upper halves of words. These are our directives, our signposts towards meaning.

The rest, Huey claims, is projection: a *throwing forward* of content by a consciousness that has been trained to plausibly fill in the gaps. The rest, in other words, we make up.

I was and remain struck by these findings.

The suggestion that reading involves projection as much as reception, making things up about the written facts of the world as much as receiving them phrased and printed, was the starting point for the workshop. I wanted to design an exercise that could slow this process down, pause it, delay it—in order to make it manifest to ourselves. To turn what we experience as a minor problem (misreading, unknowingly correcting and so failing to see my own mistakes) into a resource.

An everyday phenomenon to think with: If a substantial part of reading is, necessarily, something like educated guess-work, then how are we trained to guess? How might we train ourselves to guess otherwise?

scanned pages of this story on this elaborate eye-tracking set-up, I was very self-conscious. You can see in the line that I'm really trying to read everything: every single word. Until, that is, I get caught up in the story. A few pages into my reading, the line my eye makes suddenly gets more open, looser, faster. There is this incredible sentence in a book by philosopher Hélène Cixous called *Three Steps on the Ladder of Writing* where she talks about reading as "an escape in broad daylight." You think I'm here, but actually I'm somewhere else. And it feels like this line (Figure 2.) is showing how I start to go somewhere else: my reading gets faster and freer and I seem to be starting to forget the weird context that I was in.

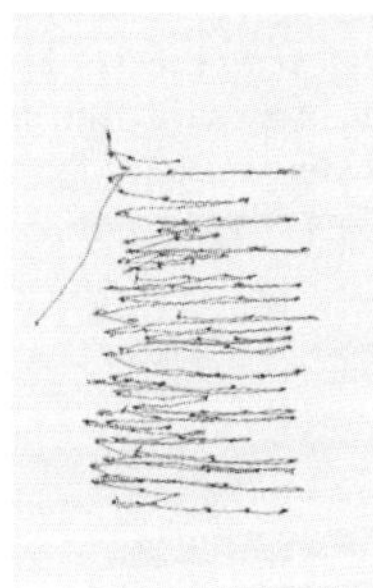

FIGURE 2

I had made this eye-drawing, the trace of the movements my eyes had made over the twenty-one pages of story, but without the source text that was directing the line (and of course how the story had been type-set on the page played a big part in this) it didn't really make sense to me. It mattered that I had been reading Henry James, and that I had been reading this text and not any other. So I decided to present it like this, as having my reading overwrite the story.

This was interesting to me because reading as an action doesn't tend to leave a lot of traces, so here was the original text marked by my passage over or through it. I liked looking at the line of my reading overwriting James's writing. But I was even more curious to see where my eyes were resting, and why they were touching certain words more than others. What portion of the text had my eyes actually seen, and what parts had I been filling in, or making up?

FIGURE 3

Sam helped me to analyze this first paragraph of my reading and the image (Figure 3.) and a new text emerged on the basis of where my eyes paused, indicated by these dots, and the words it returned to—the title my reading gave me was *Story the Story in It*.

And that was where the project stopped—the final stage was to write about it, in an essay I have been quoting to you from.[1] I had gathered all this material but realized that,

An everyday phenomenon to think with, and perhaps also to write with: If reading is a speculative action we perform on a text, prompted but not ever wholly determined by the words on the page, how might we document this process? What new forms of reading and writing might we imagine to evidence and extend this process? And what new questions might they raise, or practices of reading and writing might they produce?

[EVERYONE GETS PENS AND PAPER]

For the exercise of today, I altered two different types of text. You will see that they have different fonts and are laid out very differently on the page. Following Huey's insights into how little we need our eyes to take in when we read, I've altered them in such a way to give you the first half of the words, sometimes only the first letter, sometimes the first two. I want to invite you first to read these texts—which have so much missing—and then to write them in. Or, to put it another way, to make them up. The exercise is not about finding the right answer, unearthing what the texts originally said, but about projecting, writing them forward. If we take this idea of reading as a throwing forward seriously, what would you write on the basis of these small indications, these word-parts? So you can't get it wrong—what will be interesting will be what new pieces of writing we make on the basis of where these prompts for reading point us but what I would insist on is to project a text that makes sense to you. It can't simply be nonsense, though you can and will of course bring your own criteria to what you think it means to make a piece of writing make sense.

1 Kate Briggs, "Story the Story in It," *Amodern 6: Reading the Illegible* (July 2016) https://amodern.net/article/story-the-story-in-it/.

The final part of the workshop will be to arrive at consensus with each other, to compare what you have each written on the basis of these scores, to work towards corroborating your pieces of writing—until we arrive at versions that make sense for all of us. I realize the exercise is wholly artificial. I mean—it is clearly not possible, in everyday reading, for us to separate out what the eye sees and what the brain processes, to delay and try to expose ourselves to this work of projecting. But I wonder what questions doing this will open up?

from one point of view, all I had done was undertake an elaborate process in order to get to, or in order to allow myself to get to, the point of writing a new piece of writing. If I wanted to write a short story, I asked myself: Why not just write a short story? This has a lot to do with my own path towards authorship. It seems that I did and sometimes still do need to take an elaborate detour in order to give myself permission to write. But this also relates to why I find translation so interesting, productive and important: like this eye-tracking project, it tricks me out of my own habits, my own preparedness, to bring me somewhere I would have not arrived at alone, left to my own devices.

Ag t ro .
T win .
H sta
T cra . pa
Gre li
H sta

A ag t ro
T win
H sta a t win
A kn a t do
H tu
T kn i rep
H wa
Fac t do , h wa
T do op . I sl op
I i h s .
H sta i t do
H sa :—S .
H clo t do be hi , sta wi
hi ba t t do lo ro
H whi .—S , h sa ag
—H a se .

Ea fa sin 20 , wil bio Jor Ric ha ret t t sa port o t Cli Ri i Ten , bra fo t wor – te o tho o ne de mus sh gle , fr t sur o t wat .

T ma di -o is recog a fi . Bu on Ric se t fi fresh mus , wh lo qu dif t th mar co o mo fri fa , h sc t ri a fi an ev fi t 1 sec .

“T sm wi kn yo o yo fe ,” Ric sa . “Y se wh w a hea loo ri b no the ju de bod sca ever .”

Participant: It really felt like a confrontation with myself, also with what is going on inside of me at the moment.

Kate: Yes, and this is in line with why Freud was so interested in misreading. If you find certain motives or images repeating, you can think of how and why this relates to you—what this says about your readiness to read roses rather than rooms, for example.

What I found interesting is that when I prepared the texts, and then I looked at them again later, I had this moment of defamiliarization where I couldn’t see back to the prior version anymore. I had forgotten what the original words were, and so was forced, like you, to think forwards.

P: It would’ve been very different to look at the texts for only two seconds, not writing anything, and then discuss what they are about. Because I find hotspot points in this. I see Cl… and Clinton flashes up, and Climate. And based on that a whole story comes up in my mind, but when I have to fill in every word it becomes like trying to get a crossword right, and then I’m already beyond the idea that there is an actual situation in the world that I should “get.”

Kate: That priming, like a first glimpse and then speculating upon a possible story, and the one or two directions your brain immediately goes in, reminds me a bit of predictive texting. You know, when you’re writing messages and the algorithm suggests a path for your sentence. I’m interested in the degree in which we are oriented to go where we are able to go. What are the broader, bigger structures and powers that are pointing you towards Clinton and not —I don't know—Clouds? We were talking about some of you feeling freer and more enabled to make decisions by one of the texts,—the more poem-like one—and that then having an influence on how you feel about the exercise. It's fascinating how that priming—the sense of okay, I know what this is, this allows me to write this rather than that—happens in all circumstances all the time. Who is free of that? Surely this relates to how our readiness to receive the facts of the world is dependent on our backgrounds, our cultures, educations, languages, as well as how those facts are presented to us. I hope this exercise brings us up against this.

But I'd like to push a bit further on what are we talking about when we are talking about speculation? I was bringing it down in a way by defining it as guesswork…

P: You could argue against defining speculation as guessing, by saying that in guessing you hold onto the same rules of meaning-making while speculation tries to go beyond that.

Kate: I'm curious to know what it means for you to make something that you feel makes sense. In the context of poetry, it could make sense to write something that has its own, new coherence. I wanted the sense-making process to be part of the exercise.

P: That seems to be the crucial tension: how to stretch our idea of what makes sense, and how much this needs to still be attached to what makes sense to us already.

Kate: This for me comes together in the relationship between reconstruction and projection. And how, in the exercise what feels like a reconstruction can actually be a projection, and the other way around. You are not, in fact, excavating existing meaning—you are necessarily making it. And for me, maybe also because I brought Freud into the room, psychoanalysis is hugely interesting in relation to this. When you, for example, receive the information of a dream, and the idea that it might be possible to extrapolate this back to a specific meaning, the source or original cause of the dream, but how—

in Freud's account—this extrapolation is always, in fact, an interpretation, a translation, in other words a new story. It doesn't take us backwards to the source of the dream, or it doesn't ever straightforwardly do that, it must also take us forwards to a story, that is not the source, which is probably unrecoverable. The two operations—recovery and projection—maybe being almost the same thing or intertwining, and how this then relates to the way you have been making propositions for new sentences: working with what these words might once have meant, or been part of, and at the same time thinking forward to what they *could* now mean.

P: I was constantly focusing on what these words *wanted* to mean. It almost became a question of "who is your contract with?" Because there is the possibility of finding the contract between these bits and you, trying to create something together, and then there is the contract with the origin to which these parts belong to. In my head, it was very clear that my contract was with these bits of words and this gave me a feeling of direction.

Kate: The relationship with translation seems very alive here. For me, when translating the key question is always: to whom or what am I responsible? The question of how to negotiate my responsibility when representing someone else's work is configured each time anew in a way that is very context-specific.

You asked earlier: What shared and familiar grounds need to be established for meaningful speculation to happen? Contract is a very nice word in this regard, which relates to the action of world-making. What kind of contract do you make with the reader? And how?

Speculation might be the move of reaching towards what *could* work, to then checking that against the available evidence, and then reaching again and moving back. Reaching-checking-reaching-checking, on the basis of what you allow yourself to do, to whom or what you feel responsible and with whom you have a contract. That sounds very much like translation to me.

Were some of you surprised or excited by the sentences you produced?

P: I think because we have been talking about facts here, a sentence like "facts tainting dogma" came out; which is funny because it's basically about the truth getting in the way of belief rather than the other way around.

Kate: Yes, these methods where you trick yourself into writing something that you haven't yet thought, then you have something on your page and you can think, "Ah now I can think with this and do something more with it."

P: Do you want to tell us what the original text was?

Kate: I think it's good to never know and just stay with the new ground that we've made. If I would share it with you, then there would be two true texts from which all the other ones you've written deviate. And to me it's much more interesting to decide amongst ourselves which of your new texts have a kind of plausibility, or interest, or coherence, or truth-like quality and which not. This to me is something that comes forward often in, for example, writing fiction. If you write fiction or literature more generally, the point is you can write anything, anywhere. But in relation to this contract, you can ask yourself: on the basis of what, what kind of internal rationale supports this thing I've written? If I can write anything at all, why *this* and not anything else? What gives it a quality of truth or necessity? I don't mean that in relation to established truths in the world, but to an agreement of this that counts, for now, as truth with the reader. And often it happens, it happened in some of the texts now, there is a sort of internal coherence. Trust comes into it then as well, making people, readers, willing to go with it. That is the question: what is generative of that willingness to be transported?

Maryam Monalisa Gharavi

THE MAYAKOVSKY FOOTNOTES: One Day I'll Teach You How to Shoot a Gun

The following is excerpted from *The Book of Disbelonging*, in a section tentatively called *American Letters. Disbelonging* is a work of experimental fiction engaging the epistolary form with the experience of the United States of America through the eyes of selected travelers, immigrants, and "alien" outsiders. The correspondences address the point of contact between epistles and history. Each letter is comprised of original compositions—or fictional enactments—germinating from extensive archival research. The method is initially forensic before turning over to a new speculative landscape for each epistle. I experiment with wide ranges of style and era-appropriate language, intrigued by the urgency and contingency of an authorial "voice" so present in the subjects' letters but evasive in their formal writing.

The book conceptually invokes the reverse of the seal of the United States, *E pluribus unum* (out of many, one) to pose instead, *Ex uno, plures*: Out of one, many. In doing so, *American Letters* tests the legibility of modern "America" as both the seat of a growing empire and a fragmentary, disintegrating entity. The experiences distilled within the letters remit the real and symbolic power of this America, from Lorca witnessing the stock market crash of 1939 to von Richthofen (and her husband, D.H. Lawrence) being denied a U.S. passport. In letters on/about the United States, these writers were concerned as much with the decomposition of an aborted fetus outside a Detroit hospital (Kahlo) as with the slow decomposition of the state (Conrad).

In the following telegrams, the Soviet poet and artist Vladimir Mayakovsky (b. 1893 in Baghdati, Georgia) corresponds from his first and only visit to North America, originating at the Mexico-U.S. borderlands. The primary text I used as research for writing these fictional telegrams is *My Discovery of America* (*Moe otkrytie Ameriki*), published in 1926. It is a lean, astonishing book ruminating on the visit, and it is more than just a travelogue.

Why did Mayakosky come to the United States? Unlike his predecessors Vladimir Korolenko (1893) and Maxim Gorky (1906), who toured America out of a curiosity to see the Chicago World's Fair (Korolenko) or in opposition to the Soviet regime (Gorky), Vladimir Mayakovsky came to America as an "unabashed publicity agent for his fatherland, transformed as it was by the

October Revolution, [arriving] more or less clandestine revolutionary, coming partly to assess the chances for a proletarian revolution in this country." So while Mayakovsky was not the first cultural ambassador (or detractor) from his country, he was, as Charles Moser has observed, "in the vanguard of an entirely new breed of Russian visitor."[1]

The U.S. was very unknown to the Soviets in 1925. I am interested in *My Discovery of America* not only for the material it offered Mayakovsky upon his return to the Soviet Union (as the basis of newspaper articles, lectures, and other forms of public reckoning) but primarily as a vehicle of address about an entirely different modality of public life than the one experienced in his home country. If Mayakovsky's poetic reflections, unvarnished criticisms, and underrated comedic sentences offer one thing, it is a clarity about the ways life was experienced in a capitalist nation-state of millionaires and paupers, one where the lives of marginalized groups shamed the spirit of equality engendered in its motto.

Mayakovsky's voice, as poetic as it is authoritative, belies a seeker who belongs neither to his increasingly repressive state of origin nor the one whose language and customs are alienating and overwhelming. But in the gap between this disbelonging lies a cautious optimism, sharing a feeling-tone with the act of speculation itself.

—Maryam Monalisa Gharavi

1 Charles A. Moser, "Mayakovsky and America," *The Russian Review* 25, no. 3 (July 1966): 243.

2 The following are telegrams written by Vladimir Mayakovsky written by me. Although I notarize that they are entirely fictional, they rely on a valuable primary source (Mayakovsky's own book) and secondary-source scholarship on/about Mayakovsky's journey.

I also consulted historical data such as weather patterning, land use certificates, and almanacs to determine a range of sensorial possibilities on the specific dates the telegrams were "written."

Here we are, in the footnotes of this text within a text. As the lowest-rung bottom within the technology of a book or text, footnotes are viewed as interstitial at best, the "in the weeds" at worst. I have a preference for margin notes, though they may not fare much better there, existentially speaking. Either way you're either under someone's shoe or edged away from the main town square.

Yet I view these marginalized footnotes as a plausible portal of expansion into the speculative element of the Mayakovsky letters. Their aim is both demystification—revealing to the reader the underbelly of some of the research behind these fictions—as well as the vitalization of play. We walk the streets of fiction assuredly; may we also place our footfall on the cobbled ground in the hope of loitering there.

◆

Three Western Union telegrams[2] from Vladimir Mayakovsky to Lilya Yuryevna Brik. Though he is not known to have sent letters from his travels to the Western Hemisphere, Mayakovsky corresponded with Brik, with whom he shared an intellectual and romantic relationship (including during her marriage to Osip Brik), via the telegraph service after entering the United States. He first entered at Laredo, the largest inland port of entry at the Mexico-U.S. border. After previously being denied a permit, he was admitted as an advertising artist. Thereafter he travels northward via train to St. Louis, Philadelphia, and New York.

3 Though he visited only once, Mayakovsky's journey to North America was a momentous occasion in his life. We know that as early as September 1923 he was making U.S. visa queries, to no avail. He postponed his trip on multiple occasions as a result.

With a steamship ticket in hand, he departed for Mexico with the intention of visiting it even if he were not allowed entry into the U.S.

As Charles Moser notes, "He never visited England or Italy." *

* Charles A. Moser, "Mayakovsky's Unsentimental Journeys," *The American Slavic and East European Review*, vol 19, no. 1, (February 1960): 85.

4 Mayakovsky's love for her has largely been described as incandescent, as he "fell wildly and melodramatically in love with Lili."

One of the challenges of this letter is that Mayakovsky's New York experience remains murky. We know that he "fathered a child with a Russian émigré—a dangerous secret." *

* Sophie Pinkham, "When were you thinking of shooting yourself?" *London Review of Books*, vol 39, no.1 (February 6, 2017) accessed www.lrb.co.uk

5 Mayakovsky produced six poems on the sea, en route to Mexico. After gaining admission to the U.S. as an advertising artist, he essentially censored his own work. "In order to avoid possible unpleasantness he obliterated the most iconoclastic and revolutionary phrases in the texts of those poems he carried with him." Moser, 91.

6 Lili Brik paid for a new set of teeth for Mayakovsky, which by age twenty "were already rotten stumps; he smoked a hundred cigarettes a day." Pinkham.

7 "In 1920, Mayakovsky wrote a verse epic that began, '150,000,000 is the name of the author of this poem,' identifying himself with the population of Russia. He pretended to submerge his voice in the collective, though the tone remained unmistakably his own." Pinkham.

TELEGRAM NO. 4

Hamilton Hotel
Laredo (Mexico)[3]

28 July 1925

TO: LILI BRIK
Moscow, U.S.S.R.

MY LILECHKA[4]

I WAS SO DEJECTED AFTER THE FIRST BAN[5] ON ENTRY THAT I DID NOT REALIZE THEY GAVE ME A SIX-MO. VISA UNTIL AFTER WE CROSSED THE CROSSING AT LAREDO. I WAS TOO TIRED TO EXAMINE IT CLOSELY BUT A FELLOW RUSSIAN HELD IT UP TO THE LIGHT. LITTLE MONEY AND LITTLE ENGLISH HERE BUT I AM MAKING UP PHRASES FROM THE SOUNDS.

IMMEDIATELY BEGAN SEARCHING FOR CIGARETTES.[6] FOUND MODIANOS, AVOIDED LUCKY STRIKES AND THE NERMAS WITH EGYPTIAN ADVERTISEMENT.

VERY HUNGRY AND TIRED WE[7] ENDED UP ON CHIHUAHUA STREET, WHERE PROPER IRRIGATION IS STILL A MYTH. STREET PUDDLES INTERCHANGE WITH OUTHOUSES AND MY FEET SANK INTO GRAY FILTH. BEER IS CHEAP. BUT MEXICAN LABOR IS CHEAP TOO.

8 Re: Osip/Lili: "Lili took lovers openly throughout the marriage. Unorthodox sexual and domestic arrangements formed part of the period's experiments with the place of women in society and the family once traditional marriage had been rejected as a manifestation of capitalist property rights and an instrument of women's oppression." Pinkham.

NO ONE CAN SAY FOR SURE HOW MANY KLAN MEMBERS LIVE IN THE STATE OF TEXAS. I HAVE HEARD ONE HUNDRED THOUSAND, OR THREE HUNDRED THOUSAND, AT ANY GIVEN MOMENT. THEY CLAIM TO BE CHIEFLY CONCERNED WITH THE RESTORATION OF LAW AND ORDER. LAW AND ORDER, AS THOUGH EVERYWHERE THEY STEP IS NOT MARKED BY LAWLESSNESS AND CHAOS. THE FUNDAMENTAL CHRISTIANS DO NOT BELIEVE IN EVOLUTED MONKEYS, ONLY AN ABSENTED GOD.

MY LOVE TO OSIA[8]

YOUR

Volodya //

(collect)

9 He spoke Georgian and Russian and nothing else. "In large measure, foreign lands remained closed to [Mayakovsky] because of his inability to speak any Western language, as a result of which he had to remain among Russian émigré groups during most of his time abroad." Moser, 98.

10 Mayakovsky's *The Bedbug* premiered in 1929. Difficult to summarize, the play centers on Ivan Prisypkin, a former Party member, who is accidentally frozen in 1922 inside an economic system, the New Economic Policy (NEP), that would include "a free market and capitalism, both subject to state control," while socialized state enterprises would operate on "a profit basis." Vladimir Mayakovsky, *The Bedbug and Selected Poetry, The World Publishing Company*, trans. Max Hayward and George Reavey (1960).

11 Much like Friedrich Engels' famed automation anxiety in the nineteenth century, Mayakovsky "may have begun to suspect that a certain dehumanization of man is an inevitable aspect of a machine culture," citing the exhaustion of Ford assembly workers. Moser, 99.

TELEGRAM NO. 5

Laredo (Mexico)
telegraph office

29 July 1925

TO: LILI BRIK
Moscow, U.S.S.R.

LILECHKA

I KNEW BETTER THAN TO ASK OUTRIGHT FOR GIN AND WHISKEY. INSTEAD I LEARNED HOW TO PRONOUNCE MOONSHINE, WITH EMPHASIS ON *OO* SO IT CAME OUT OF MY MOUTH AS MUUUNSHEN[9]. SURPRISINGLY STRONG! WITH THE EFFECT OF NICOTINE OR CAFFEINE. IT KEPT ME AWAKE UNTIL FOUR O'CLOCK IN THE MORNING, THOUGH A RUSSIAN STORE OWNER CLAIMED MY SLEEPLESSNESS MAY BE CAUSED BY THE CONSTANT ILLUMINATION.

FEW ARE BOTHERED BY ILLEGAL ALCOHOL OR LOW WAGES FOR A FULL DAY'S WORK[10]. THE FOUNDRY WORKERS ARE ON STRIKE. THE LONGSHOREMEN ARE ON STRIKE. BUT NO ONE IS ON STRIKE IN THE OIL OR PETROLEUM JOBS, OR EVEN AUTOMOBILES. THE TEMPORARY WORKERS ARE MEXICAN, BLACK, OR WHITE, AND ALL OF THEM MOVE THROUGH THE STREETS LIKE BIRDS WHO HAVE FORGOTTEN THEY CAN MAKE GOOD USE OF WINGS.[11]

THE TRAIN LEAVES IN THE EARLY MORNING FOR NEW YORK—VIA PITTSBURGH, WHERE WE MAY HOP OFF FOR A FEW DAYS AND MEET SYNDICATE WORKERS. BETTER TO TAKE THIS TRIP THAN BUY A DIRECT TICKET.

YOUR

V. //

(collect)

12 Mayakovsky's *My Discovery of America* is neatly divided into four parts: "Mexico," "New York," "America," and "Departure." The New York chapter begins with his interaction at the American consulate:

"'Moscow. That's in Poland?'
'No,' I replied, 'it's in the U.S.S.R.'
This made no impression.
I was given my visa." *

> * Vladimir Mayakovsky, *My Discovery of America* Trans. Neil Cornwell (London: Hesperus Press, [1926] 2005).

13 Before his trip to Mexico Mayakovsky's hotel room was burglarized: "I'm not too sorry about... the money. But the thought that my journey might be cut short and that I might have to come home again like an idiot completely enraged me." Moser, 91.

TELEGRAM NO. 12

Manhattan (New York)[12] 4 September 1925
Hotel Wolcott, 4 West 31st Street

TO: LILI BRIK
Moscow, U.S.S.R.

LI-LI-BRI

EARLY AUTUMN CHILL ON THIS NEW YORK ISLAND. JACKET INSUFFICIENT AND CRUMBLING. A SHORT BALDING FRENCHMAN WHO WAS HERE DURING THE HEATWAVE OF JUNE, WHICH KILLED ALMOST 25, STRIKES UP A CONVERSATION WITH ME THROUGH AN INTERPRETER, A JEWISH SHOP OWNER. "THE COOL AIR IS FINE AND WELCOME!" THE GRAY STORM WAVES OVERHEAD LOOK PUNISHING.

THE WOLCOTT HOTEL ADVERTISES ITS LOCATION ON "A QUIET STREET — NO CROSSTOWN TRAFFIC." BUT TODAY, A FRIDAY EVENING, THERE IS THE LOW RUMBLE OF STREETCARS AND THE HUM OF PAPER-SELLERS. I PULLED A PILLOW OVER MY HEAD AT 4:00 A.M., DISTURBED BY REAL OR IMAGINED COCKS.

LIKE A GRANNY, I HAVE STOWED AWAY SOME COINS AND OTHER MONIES UNDERNEATH MY MATTRESS.[13] THE ROOM IS $3.00 FOR ROOM AND BATH PER DAY, A LITTLE EXTRA FOR PRESSED SHIRTS AND TROUSERS. I AM PARTAKING,

14 Sophie Pinkham characterizes Mayakovsky as "certainly squeamish, a hypochondriac and germophobe," possibly due to his father's death by blood poisoning from an infected needle. From Pinkham I deduced the detail that Mayakovsky would not rely on New York hotel bathtubs for his cleanliness, preferring to travel with his own wares, as when she writes: "He avoided public transport, handshakes and doorknobs; always carried his own soap and drinking cup; and traveled with a folding rubber bathtub."

15 In terms of appearance, Mayakovsky was over six feet tall, and said to lower everyone "like a storm cloud." Mayakovsky, *The Bedbug and Selected Poetry*, 19.

16 Prisypkin is put "in a deep freeze after an accident in 1929 and revived in 1979, by which point 'Roses are found only in gardening books, and dreams only in medical books, in the chapter on hallucinations.'"* With him is a bedbug, "which goes on to spread obsolete illnesses like love, romance, poetry, suicide, dancing, smoking, and drinking. In the end Prisypkin and the bedbug are caught and put in a zoo. Mayakovsky told the actor playing Prisypkin to imitate his own mannerisms. It's hard not to conclude that he'd given up on utopian dreams and his hopes of using poetry to foment a spiritual revolution.

> * After fifty years, he is revived in a world that looks very different. Around him is an ideal communist world, almost a utopia. There is no more poverty and destitution, illness and natural disasters have been defeated, and people have forgotten about drunkenness, smoking, and swearing. Prisypkin does not belong in this future. Mayakovsky, *The Bedbug*.

17 One of the difficulties of this telegrammed letter is that Mayakovsky's New York experience remains murky, even tragic. We know that he "fathered a child with a Russian emigre—a dangerous secret." Pinkham. We also know that an upstate leisure trip "ended tragically with the drowning of his New York host, Isaiah Hoorgin." Moser, 93.

18 Perhaps even the resolute iconoclast Mayakovsky harbored an American dream, of sorts. First, it lay buried in the deferral of ever visiting the U.S., given several frustrating years of attempts at a visa. Secondly it "may have been a prime factor in the creation of a certain disillusionment with Soviet life which attacked him before his suicide." Moser, 90.

19 Not unlike his difficulties entering the U.S., Mayakovsky faced difficulties exiting the Soviet Union years later in the autumn of 1929. He was categorically denied permission by his government to go abroad. This travel ban plunged him into defeat, even suicidal despair.

BECAUSE EVERY INCH OF MY CLOTHES FEEL SOILED AFTER EVEN A MODEST EVENING WALK.

THE HOTEL ADVERTISES A “POWERFUL SUCTION CLEANER” DRAWING OUT DUST ON EVERY INCH OF THE PLACE, BUT I BATHE IN MY FOLDING RUBBER BATHTUB [14] THE MINUTE I AM BACK IN MY ROOM. THE PORTER WHO PICKED UP MY SHIRT THIS MORNING ASKED IF I WAS “HAPPY” WITH HIS SERVICE AND I COULD DO NOTHING BUT NOD IMPOTENTLY AND SAY “KHEPPY! HOWWW... KHEPPY!” THE TOP OF MY HEAD BUMPED THE CEILING AS I SAID IT [15]. EVERY TIME I OPEN MY MOUTH COMMEDIA DELL’ARTE EXITS! WALKING MOVIE SLAPSTICK!

I WROTE A SCRIBBLE OF A POEM [16] TODAY AFTER A BREAKFAST OF COLD EGGS AND DILUTED COFFEE.

LILECHKA, I SWEAR TO KNOW NOTHING OF THE FAMED NEW YORK [17] SPEED AND REGULARITY, EASE AND COOLHEADEDNESS. CHAOS EMITS FROM EVERY CAR LANE AND TRUNDLING BUS LINE. THEY COMPETE WITH A HORDE OF THOUSANDS ON FOOT FOR TRUNCATED SPACE ON GRAVEL AND CONCRETE. BUT ONWARD [18] IN KNOWING IT I GO [19].

EVER

V. //

(collect)

Figure 1. Detail of a photograph of Mayakovsky after his return from the U.S. in December 1925.

Federico Campagna & the Department of Speculative Facts

Metaphysics for Everybody

Diagrams by Federico Campagna, text by the Department of Speculative Facts, recollected from a lecture at the Jan Van Eyck Academy and written for readers of all ages.

Our thoughts are like a building.
What we're thinking in day-to-day life
is on the top floor.

But there's a floor below.
That's politics, or in other words;
our assumptions about the world.
Even when we don't realize it,
these assumptions are shaping our thoughts.

So have we got to the bottom of it all?
Not yet.
Even below that floor there is another layer:
Metaphysics.

What is metaphysics?
What we believe about the nature of reality.
What we can and can't know,
how we got here.
The big questions!

So metaphysics is the base of the building.
It shapes our politics.
And then our politics shapes our thoughts.

Religions offer us metaphysics.
But you can also make your own.

When social facts
—agreements about what is true—
come in to question,
it's important to have a healthy and self-aware
metaphysics underlying our thoughts.

As an example of a metaphysics,
we will take you step by step through one
Federico Campagna made.

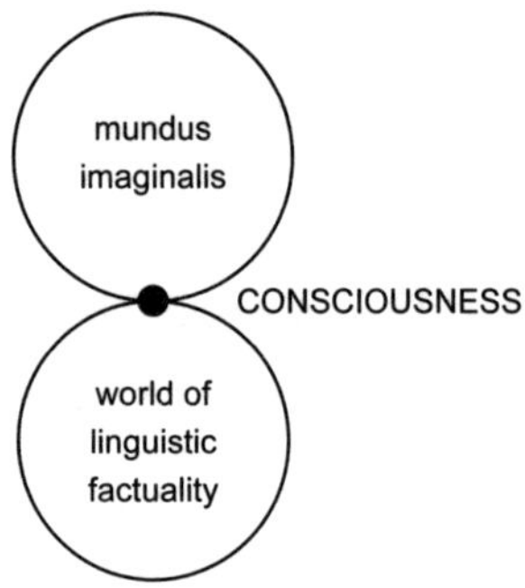
mundus imaginalis
CONSCIOUSNESS
world of linguistic factuality

Let's start with the
WORLD OF LINGUISTIC FACTUALITY:
this includes everything
we know through language and facts,
and where we live in our day-to-day life.

For some people that might be everything,
but not in Federico's system.
Above the world of words, there is
MUNDUS IMAGINALIS.
It's a term that was invented
by French philosopher, Henry Corbin,
to describe certain aspects relating
to Islamic Mysticism.

It means spirit, creativity, and feelings.
This 'country of nonwhere'
is a real place that you can always return to.
Now, in Federico's diagram the connection
between these two zones is CONSCIOUSNESS,
an awareness that looks at part of the word
and ascribes it back to itself.

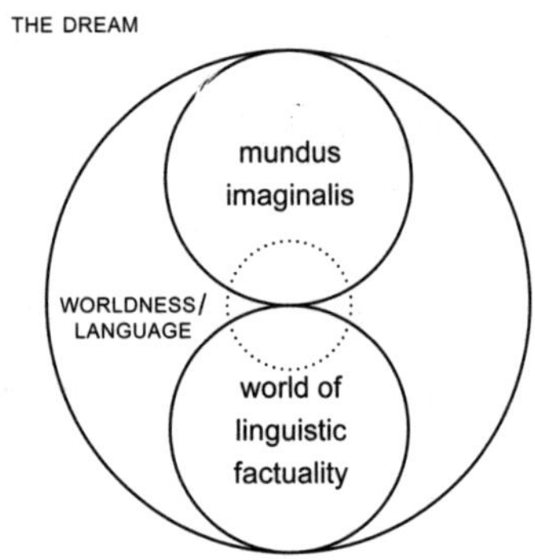
THE DREAM
mundus
imaginalis
WORLDNESS/
LANGUAGE
world of
linguistic
factuality

What we're aware of in a given moment
is just a small area of things traveling
between these first two circles.

Everything that *can* fit in these two circles
—more than just one moment
of CONSCIOUSNESS—
that's the realm of
WORLDLINESS AND LANGUAGE.

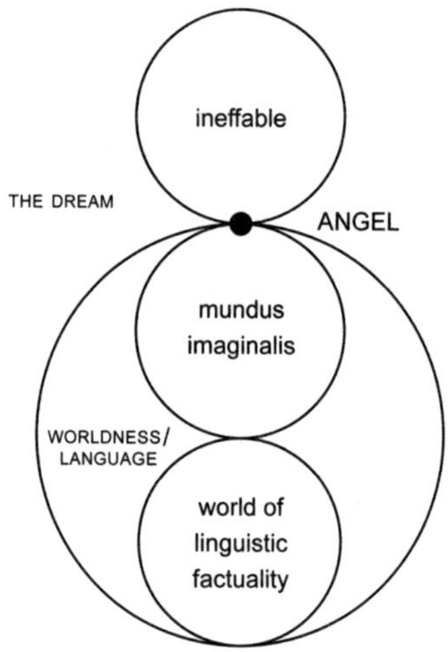
ineffable
THE DREAM
ANGEL
mundus
imaginalis
WORLDNESS/
LANGUAGE
world of
linguistic
factuality

So is that it?
Not yet.

On top of this in-between-place
of the MUNDUS IMAGINALIS,
there is the INEFFABLE.
That's what we feel is there,
but we don't have words or evidence for it
—it's too big to be described.
So how does that come into
our CONSCIOUSNESS then?
It needs a very special type of messenger between
the INEFFABLE and
THE WORLD OF LANGUAGE:

THE ANGEL.

Angels are a figure in many religions,
but you don't need to be religious
to see their function.

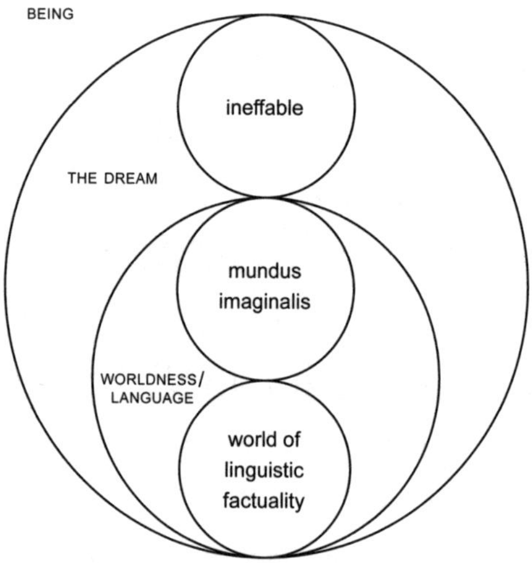
BEING
ineffable
THE DREAM
mundus imaginalis
WORLDNESS/ LANGUAGE
world of linguistic factuality

So in Federico's system,
all of this fits into the realm
of THE DREAM.
But of course, there's more.

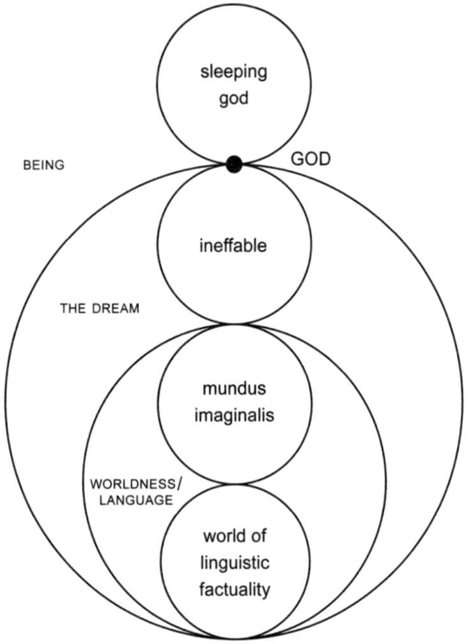
sleeping god
GOD
BEING
ineffable
THE DREAM
mundus imaginalis
WORLDNESS/ LANGUAGE
world of linguistic factuality

The next circle is
the SLEEPING GOD.

Why is god asleep?
Because there's so much of god, so many
unknown and inactive parts.
Only a little bit of that trickles down
to where we can fathom it,
in the zone of the INEFFABLE.
That little bit of SLEEPING GOD
that we can sense is called (to Federico)
just regular GOD.

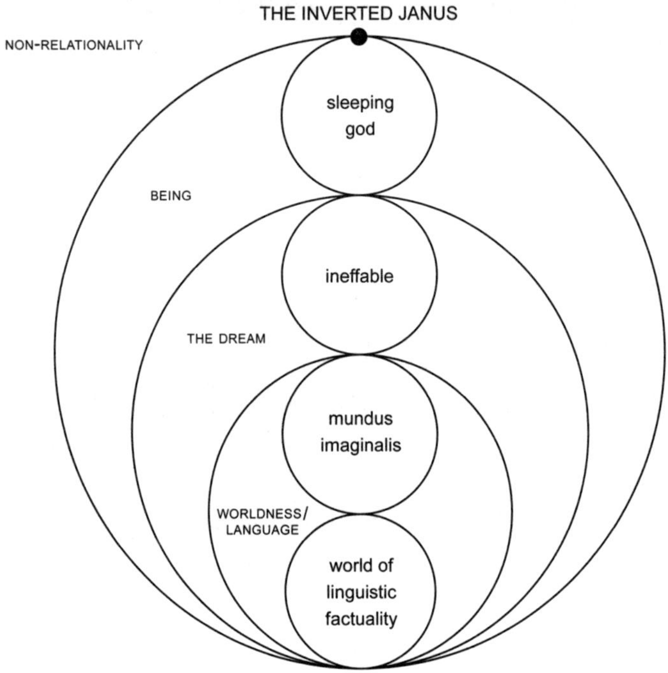
THE INVERTED JANUS
NON-RELATIONALITY
sleeping god
BEING
ineffable
THE DREAM
mundus imaginalis
WORLDNESS/ LANGUAGE
world of linguistic factuality

So with SLEEPING GOD included,
we have the circle of BEING,
which includes everything that is.
On the other side of BEING is
NON-RELATIONALITY.

So how do we go outside of BEING?
Through the INVERTED JANUS.
Janus is from Roman mythology, the god of
doors, passageways and beginnings.
Janus has two faces, looking both
forward and backward.

We can imagine INVERTED JANUS
having two backs of heads,
not-facing everywhere!

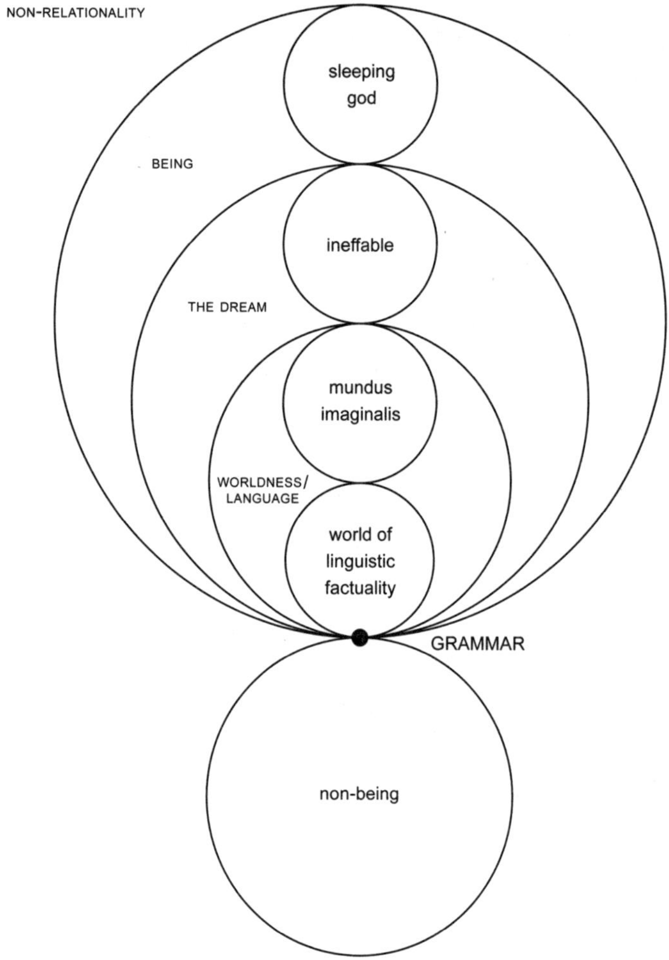
NON-RELATIONALITY
sleeping
god
BEING
ineffable
THE DREAM
mundus
imaginalis
WORLDNESS/
LANGUAGE
world of
linguistic
factuality
GRAMMAR
non-being

There's another thing outside of BEING
we shouldn't forget about:
NON-BEING.
Everything that isn't.

Unlike NON-RELATIONALITY,
NON-BEING is easier to grasp.
We can bring it directly into our
WORLD OF LINGUISTIC factuality.

How?
With GRAMMAR.
The way we arrange words and
make sentences, can bring something
from NON-BEING into BEING.
Federico sees the function of GRAMMAR
as that of the DEVIL.

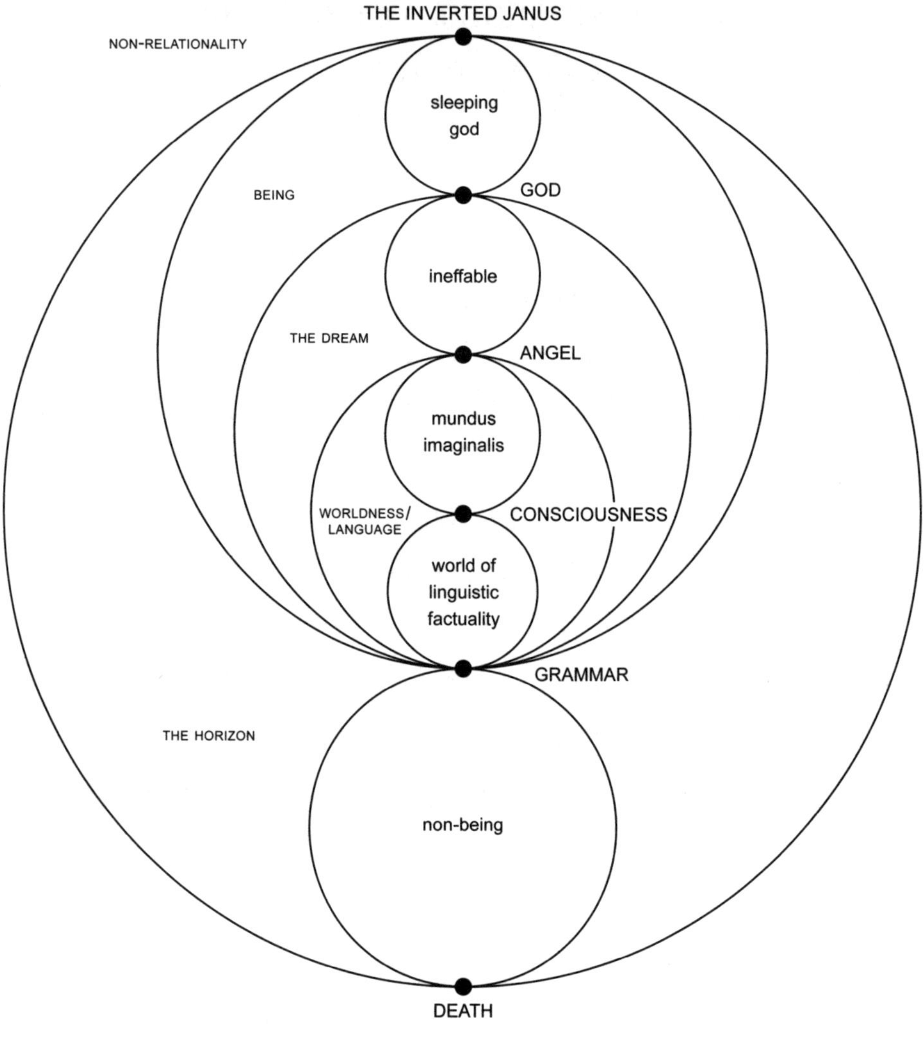
THE INVERTED JANUS
NON-RELATIONALITY
sleeping god
BEING
GOD
ineffable
THE DREAM
ANGEL
mundus imaginalis
WORLDNESS/ LANGUAGE
CONSCIOUSNESS
world of linguistic factuality
GRAMMAR
THE HORIZON
non-being
DEATH

So all of NON-BEING and BEING
together makes the HORIZON,
which is as far as you can see,
or the furthest point
you can imagine and travel towards.

On the other side of that is
NON-RELATIONALITY.
We don't even know if there is anything
in NON-RELATIONALITY
(maybe there isn't) and we will only find out
after DEATH.

By the way, now's a good time to tell you about SPECULATIVE PHILOSOPHY:
It says "just because you can't see something, doesn't mean it's not there."

It takes you beyond the existing
and human-centered way of seeing.
How do your pets see the world?
How does the grass see the soil?

The systems for structuring
what you *can't* see are called metaphysics,
and they completely shape your thinking
about what you can see!

When news sources and politicians say
all sorts of conflicting things,
it's important to learn and be aware
of the metaphysics structuring truth.

So now you've learned
a little about Federico's system,
you can try to make your own!

Tristan Garcia

Everything Exists!

I

What is DISRADICALISM?
It is URGENT to KNOW

DISRADICALISM: because the world is MULTIPLE
Why would it be created just ONE TIME?:
Proclaim that all belief is JUST and JUSTIFIED
Because All IS
The Christian God and the Mahometan God
The God of the Savages and the God of the Civilized
The world was and wasn't created
The BIBLE is right! DARWIN is right!

God exists AND God does not exist
DISRADICALISM explains EVERYTHING AND ITS OPPOSITE
Nothing is impossible
God EXISTS, God IS DEAD, God DOES NOT YET EXIST

THE CHURCH OF DISRADICALISM
Extraterrestrials! Beings from other worlds! YOU!
NOTHING is NOTHING
ALL is
Some THING
ALL is TRUE

Come and hear the IMPORTANT THINGS
You are right to BELIEVE, you are right to DOUBT
Who is WRONG? No one is WRONG!
DISRADICALISM provides ANSWERS

BUY: the ANSWERS of DISRADICALISM,
by the Reverend Prince Bennett
If you want to KNOW

(tract of 1931, private collection)

II

Who is Prince Bennett?
Here is the true story of
the man who invented 71 religions
written and illustrated by Philip Wood III
by HUMAN KNOWLEDGE EDITIONS
ages 7 and up

The grandfather of Prince Bennett was a slave. A slave is a person who is the property of another person, according to the law of the land where he lives. Slavery was abolished, but Prince Bennett's parents were very poor. They came to the city of Chicago to look for work and that is where Prince was born (see image 1).

*

Prince was very intelligent. But he was black and, at this time, blacks couldn't get an education. To earn money, he became a peddler (*image 2*). But in Europe there was a war, and Prince went to fight. He was very courageous and he saved the lives of several companions during the battle of Champagne (see image 3). He received a military medal.

*

Here, Prince Bennett poses under the Eiffel Tower (see image 4).

He discovers Paris. At that time in Europe, poets, painters, and musicians gathered together and talked about *the future* all night long: we called them the *avant-garde*. There were all sorts: *Dadaists*, *Futurists*, *Supremacists,* and *Constructivists.* Prince Bennett became friends with several Surrealists. He spoke to them about Voodoo from Haiti, and pretended that he came from there: it was a *lie* but Prince Bennett spoke well and everyone believed him! On the next page, there are several pictures of him at an important exhibition. As you can see (*image 5*), Prince Bennett is very elegant: he walks with a cane, bowtie, and bowler hat.

He discovers Nietzsche's work, which says *God is dead*. But Bennett decides to deliver several lectures in France declaring that *Nietzsche was mistaken* and that *God has not yet been born*.

*

Unfortunately, Prince Bennett runs out of money. He returns to the United States. He lives a *dissolute life*. He drinks in bars and visits women of ill repute (see image 6). In 1927 in Des Moines, he forms the *Universal Society of Education*, which changes names several times before becoming the *Church of DISRADICALISM*. This is the first religion founded by Prince Bennett. He eventually has a dozen or so disciples who meet together once a week. According to some, it isn't *serious*, but for others, it is *important*.

*

The following year, Prince Bennett disbands the group and creates the *Church of the Inexistent God*. He spends a summer traveling across Ohio, Iowa, and Texas, preaching in tents (see image 7). After having been arrested and spending time in prison for *blasphemy*, he returns to Chicago, where he edits the first issue of the *Sect of the Just-Born God*. That same year, he has *thirteen visions* in a row (see images 8, 9, and 10): he has a dream where the first man speaks to him about the last man; he communicates in sign language with a monkey and a dog; he sees the sky and the Earth switch places; he falls from the second floor of a building and falls upwards (landing on the rooftop); he meets Jesus-Christ-of-the-Negroes; he sees three suns in the middle of the night… He founds *thirteen religions* in that same year: *Church of the Children of the Living God; Sons of the Seekers of the Final Truth; Enochians of the City of Zion; Great Restoration of the Commandments; Authentic Night Watch; Jewish Falsification of the Sacred Scriptures; Society of Michael of the Thessalonians; Church of Integral Evolutionism; The Plan of Salvation of the New Day, The Truly Alive who Shall Never Die; Definitive Apostasy; Family of the World for Only One Day*; *The Late Annunciation*.

*

Afterward, Prince Bennett writes and self-publishes books on the *Church of Sovereign Humanism*, *The Great Refutation of Relativity and Marxism*, and also *The Scientific Conception of the Falseness of Everything*. None of these sects achieves the slightest success, but he becomes known in the black community as an *eccentric*.

At the age of fifty, Prince Bennett has already invented seventy religions. Impassioned by what he does, he himself types the tracts in hotel rooms (see image 11) and he hires professional illustrators to draw, for example, the metal rose in the circle of fire (see image 12), which is the symbol of the *Academy of Inflamed Consciousness*.

Unfortunately, with the rise of the Black Panthers (see image 13), a group that advocates *revolution*, Prince Bennett falls out of fashion and slips back into anonymity. *Politics* has replaced *religion*.

He goes back to being a street peddler who goes door-to-door for several years. He commits himself to a psychiatric hospital (see image 14), because he thinks he has lost his mind.

Finally, he is released and announces his project to defend the *Society for the White Supremacy of Blacks*, a Ku Klux Klan exclusively reserved for Negroes, according to him. Nobody pays it any heed.

*

Practically a vagrant, Prince Bennett is assassinated in 1969 by a *former disciple* of the *Church of DISRADICALISM,* the first of his *seventy-one religions.* Following a bar brawl in Oxford, Ohio, (see image 15), he dies of multiple stab wounds.

*

Here is the story of Prince Bennett (see image 16), a truly colorful, original, and, alas, forgotten person!

*

If you want to know more about Prince Bennett, the man who invented seventy-one religions, write to *Philip Wood III*, painter and illustrator of the *Concord*, at HUMAN KNOWLEDGE EDITIONS.

III

"Towards the Concord?"
About Jack LeRoy, creator of Prince Bennett, Philip Wood III, and Hank Johnson
The Chronicle of Arts, Sept. 17, 1989: B10.

We live in a time of uncertainty. Because we have bowed our heads to the contradictory injunction of liberal society: one must believe, and all beliefs are valid. Religions, sects and parties all discount their dogmas, and put them on sale for today's consumer, as if they were provisions in a catalog for fixing up our tiny personal insides.

This tumultuous time is also that of Jack LeRoy.

We do not know much about Jack LeRoy. Self-taught painter and illustrator, he lived all his life in a small city south of the Finger Lakes in New York State. This tall, redheaded guy apparently had a Mets baseball cap glued to his head year-round and developed a seemingly modest body of work separate from any movement or school: he never exhibited under his own name although he was cited by a handful of New York critics and artists as the forgotten genius of Americana.

Influenced by Burne Hogarth, Alex Raymond, and Harold Foster, whose adolescent anatomies he copied with the greatest of care, LeRoy got his start painting the book covers of popularized fiction and children's encyclopedias in gouache and watercolors. He then discovered the classic Perspectivist painters. During the 1960s, he produced large naive illustrations, swarming with more and more details, for a series of inexpensive books, including the following titles (they deserve to be cited!):

Lost Cities and Devoured Civilizations; 1001 Questions about Sexuality; **The Sky's the Limit: Empires and Conquests; The Fabulous Fortune of the Rockefellers;** The Invention of Surgery;

THE PEACE PIPE: THE TRUE STORY OF THE RED MAN; The Twenty-Five Bloodiest Battles of History; How to Amass Money Without Having Any; Submerged: the Story of Atlantis; The Woman with Two Vaginas; The Perverse Virgins of Hollywood; The Wife of Jesus; AKHENATON: THE PHARAOH FROM THE LOST STARS; The Terrible Sons of Heaven: a Timeline of Chinese Emperors; Adam Was Not the First!; The Sexuality of Divorcées: An Illustrated Study; The Curse of the Necropolis Sarcophagus; MARQUIS DE SADE:

THE HORRORS OF ABJECTION; IN SEARCH OF THE NORTHWEST PASSAGE; **Crusades: Where, When, How, and Why**; Conquistadors: The Gold that Drove Them Crazy; *How to Build a Bridge That Will Not Crumble*; BABUR: THE MOGHUL IN INDIA; *Shangri-La: The Soul's Heavenly Home*; **On the Fence About the Atom: The True History of the Manhattan Project**; *Socrates by Socrates*; **Hercules's Thirteenth Labor**; Censured Mythology; **The Great Wall of China: Builders' Secrets**; I Couldn't

Help Cheating On My Husband; Wonders of Australian Coral; All the Treasures of the Library of Alexandria; Pat Boone: A Legend; The Elephants of the Alps; Alexander and Aristotle: The Master and The Conqueror; Scaling Mount Everest!; The Animals That Never Existed; And Yet, It Turns: The True Story of Galileo; Masters of the Planet: Dinosaurs As You Have Never Seen Them; Ghost Towns of the West; TEOTIHUACAN: The Lake of the Indian Gods;

To The South Pole; **Travels in Time and Beyond**; *The Millenary Beauty of the Sequoias*; **In The Year 2000...**; THE DAY MAN WALKED ON MARS; **Blood Ran Red: The True Story of the October Revolution**; John Muir: Friend of Nature; *Magellan: Because the World Is Round*; **Oceans of the World: Treasures of the Abysses**; **Lesbians: A Scientific Study**

...

It is impossible to know exactly how many books Jack LeRoy illustrated during his prolific career. It is equally hard to recognize one of his drawings when you stumble upon it: as he refined his style, he learned how to imitate all the different genres and styles. Showing a certain taste for the *mise en scène* and large explicative images, filled with tens, or even hundreds, of people dispersed on fields of battle, as well as anatomical drawings and nudes of a scientific nature, LeRoy developed, little by little, the habit of signing certain commissions with a different name, thereby inventing parallel bodies of work.

(...)

Starting in the 1970s, his work took a new direction. Accumulating an unparalleled knowledge about all civilizations, great men, extraordinary adventures, and perversions of all sorts, he started to write and illustrate, on top of the commissions which he never stopped fulfilling, a "Universal History." He conceived of huge pictures and infinite lists establishing rather rash parallels between the Koguryo Kingdom, Chosŏn Korea, the Han Dynasty, and the Roman Empire, the Uruk and Ur civilizations, the Olmecs, the Malinke Empire, and, in this complete disorder, he established improbable links between religions, cults, customs and accouterments, categorizing according to 172 characteristics all the cultures he'd ever heard of. He committed himself to the project of a comprehensive description of the human noösphere.

Collector and creator, he claimed to have found a secret order in the chaos of everything that the human being had ever believed.

As he approached fifty, Jack LeRoy invented the term "Concord," in a self-published pamphlet, to denote the form of all human beliefs. The Concord was supposed to be the mysterious harmony of all human beliefs. In a frenzy of nonstop work, LeRoy gave life to several characters such as Hank Johnson, Philip Wood III, and Prince Bennett, whom he saw as precursors to his own Concord. He attributed imaginary works to them! He had Prince Bennett, one of his most surprising fantasies, invent seventy-one different religions, which he later used in his Canon of the Concord to fill in gaps in his classification system. (…) In fact, certain religions were left out of the Great Universal Concord. Some human beliefs did not exist yet, or at least, Jack LeRoy had not yet discovered them amongst the thousands of civilizations already known to him. Because the Concord must contain *all* possible beliefs, LeRoy wrote and published fictive biographies of false prophets (more or less believable) who defended one or another or several of the beliefs that did not yet exist. And so, to Bennett, a black dandy inspired by the European avant-gardes, the visionary inventor of a series of religions, he attributes the conception of DISRADICALISM (!).

At the end of his life, LeRoy accepts most of his commissioned work under the name Hank Johnson or Philip Wood III; to Wood, he reserves the Mormon drawings, and to Johnson the images of ufology groups and the esoteric and Gnostic pamphlets.

(…)

The exegesis of Jack LeRoy's work has not yet been completed, even though he died ten years ago. Art historians are split: the culmination of postmodern *kitsch* for some, the abandonment of Modernism through the archaic for others, he incarnates for certain impassioned collectors an ideal of the "authentic" artist in a world that "belongs now only to counterfeiters," as the author of the first monograph on Jack LeRoy confided.

We still can't respond to the question:

Who was he really?

A man of many facets. All day and all night for decades, Jack LeRoy, in his naive, almost childlike manner, drew Viking soldiers, biblical prophets, Assyrian kings, battles, massacres, family meals of American pilgrims, conquistadors, triceratops, pyramids, and golden statues as well as elves, naiads, kamis, gods of anger, UFOs, Atlanteans, Christs, chimeras, snake-men, Amazonians, vulvas, and cross-sections of lungs. What Diderot and d'Alembert's *Encyclopedia* was for the learned society of the European Enlightenment, Jack LeRoy's Concord was, perhaps, for the popular culture of the twentieth century. He mixes the real and the imaginary, history and fiction, science and religion, without discrimination. The Concord, this phantom cathedral, whose stained-glass glare scatters onto the pages of non-scholastic handbooks, pornographic literature, children's manuals, playing cards, pulp fiction covers, conspirators' pamphlets, and esoteric tomes, respects Prince Bennett's guidelines (and he is one version of LeRoy):

"Everything exists!"

Maybe… Jack LeRoy never expressed himself under his own name. The few brochures dedicated to the Concord, exchanged amongst admirers at auctions, are anonymous or reflect the opinions of Hank Johnson and Philip Wood III. We can read there that "the animal knows, knows the truth, because it doesn't think. Man doesn't know, he believes because he can't tell the difference between reality and what he thinks." It is certainly the conviction that guided the entire life of this elusive artist, who perhaps exists no more (but certainly not less) than his wildest creations.

But we have kept the best for last: according to the recent hypothesis of a French art historian, Jack LeRoy is, in fact, a creation himself, like Prince Bennett, Philip Wood III, Hank Johnson, and all the others. After all, who knows if Jack LeRoy was not invented by Jack LeRoy himself?

Sepake Angiama

Her Imaginary: Letter from the Future

How does she inhabit the structures of the past with visions of the future?

She was always fascinated with how her living environment had shaped her understanding of the world, how her relationship to others had conditioned her behavior, how advertising affected perceptions of class, sex and gender, how TV could project visions of the future while she watched in the present. In the last days she had been trying to find a film that had once been recommended to her by a friend. The image of a black woman airing her voice over the radio, the protagonist of the story, was captured on a film poster. Timid to embark on a mode of self-reflection, she wanted to raise questions that could awaken her own political struggle, such as those of positioning, addressing questions of race, class, gender and the role education plays in perpetuating stereotypes. Instead of scrutinizing reality she wondered how science fiction could help her create collective visions not yet seen, a memory of events that had not yet happened, a new language which had not yet been spoken. A trilogy of the "not yets." She had only recently found her voice. It was softly-spoken, calm, thoughtful and reflective. It also rarely questioned the simplest of things that have been accepted as, "that's just how it is." But now was the moment that she wanted to question everything.

747-400
©Disney© & TM Lu

Letter from the Future

Letter from the Future is a writing exercise that stems from an attempt to collapse space and the linearity of time. Like the Surrealist method of exquisite corpse, it is a collective writing exercise where each writer can only respond to the preceding sentence without knowing the rest of the story. The first writing exercise took place in the city of Montreal in January 2018 through conversations between Sepake Angiama and Pip Day which resulted in their selection of the phrase "All Good Things Must Begin," a quote from Octavia Butler. The SBC Gallery in Montreal brought together spatial elements that considered the question: What does it mean to create a space that cares for the voice? A space to listen and also to speak. The space also hosted a fictional meeting between Audre Lorde and Octavia Butler through a selection of books that dealt with science fiction, specifically written by black women, that forged new futures of intersectional feminism, social justice and architectures to inhabit.

In Alexis Pauline Gumbs', *Evidence* (a contribution to the book *Octavia's Brood*, a short story from a collection edited by Adrienne Maree Brown and Walida Imarisha), Gumbs receives letters from her future self, who is now dwelling in an era of post-Capitalism, to her past self. Her future self is describing a society where everyone grows with each other and all respect that growth, a world without money and one which is healing collectively. That future society has a common and collective practice of togetherness that is in contrast with our current social and economic structures, where togetherness is actually charged for. Her work made us examine our own imaginaries and capacities to generate narratives beyond our current sinister predicament.

These are a collection of narratives. Like letters from the future, we look for tools to articulate our own narratives for our future, as social and political imaginaries. These visions are collective. The use of these texts and the collective writing processes they emerge from are a practice aiming to mobilize our agency in imagining and articulating our own version of the real. Through the material we collected with different collaborators it is fascinating to see that the underlying infrastructure the stories are battling against is the deeply entrenched capitalist system. And even though the contributors to the stories are never asked to imagine a better or worse scenario for their narrative, the medium reveals its power to voice optimistic imaginaries.

Five Endless Fingers is another collectively written text that came out of The School of Darkness formed part of Kunstenfestivaldesarts over a period of five days in Brussels, Belgium. It inhabits the moment of darkness usually preceding a theatre performance, using that otherwise fleeting collective experience to formulate a narrative that draws from past personal stories. And finally, *Twelfth Moon* was written over WhatsApp with three people in three different locations that speculates on the conservative election win in the UK at the end of 2019.

“ALL GOOD THINGS MUST BEGIN”

Writing workshop, Montreal, 2018

Snow everywhere and the authorities have decided not to remove it. We are stuck inside.

Soon after, cities stopped removing snow at all, people remained indoors and communicated only electronically.

Amazon package delivery drones ruled the streets. After some weeks it became clear they were able to communicate directly with each other.

So the fun of it was to interfere with their communication through telepathy.

I let my mind-body melt into the dark green glitter abyss. Melting infinitely beyond the borders of the map.

The map has become absolute, irrelevant, our sense of direction informed by the hive mind of all of us who inhabit this glittering abyss. There are no borders, there is no time.

The lack of materiality is how we lost all meaning. There is no real connection to place, responsibility, or accountability. People disappear into fogs of self.

Sepake Angiama
Pip Day
Eliott de Smedt Day
Nadia Chaney
Mari.e Cornellier
Stephanie Filion
Suzanne Kite
Michael Nardone
Anahita Jamali Rad
Will Straw
Trish Toso

The Flat Earthers have declared that round earth laws no longer apply. They believe the world is flat because water remains flat when contained in a bottle or glass and does not curve.

It is true however that water has changed. It used to be shiny and transparent but now it is dark. The mystery is growing. No expert could give advice.

Accordingly, the street signs have had to be adapted. In fact, they've turned them into Cubistic-DADA sculptures that would point out confusingly which way to proceed.

Brandon is a scientist although not necessarily one of the best, when they heard of the shift they immediately called their mother to discuss what to do.

She had incredible eyes, they seemed like you were looking into vast solar systems opening up. There were stars, planets, unknown dimensions, they were for the first time so easy to reach.

Without sight, her other senses grew stronger. Touch, taste, smell, and hearing. She experienced the world in totally new and different ways.

Almost like a new species.

"I remember that story from my childhood, in which the darkness, the void, was moving faster and swallowing everything.

I've never thought about the possibility for darkness to have a speed. A self-determined speed.

I started to flow, grow and expanding as needed. Raining down on the earth, creating rivers, lending the way to the New Lives and the last remaining hope.

Nowhere was a place where light and dark were intertwined, but there were friendships with privileges and polyamorousness, like bees and flowers.

It was the best time of my life.

That's all I can tell you, that's all you can learn from life. After all, we are made of the emptiness we came from."

Brandon opened their drawer to take out the black, endless gloves. Immediately the finger tips started to entangle. They didn't like to get lost in the darkness. Five endless fingers traveling through time, one stretched out, the other four compressed at different lengths. What could they learn from them? That the expedition was doomed to fail?

The world was flat, the kilogram was not a kilogram and they, the people, could decide the future of earth.

But they don't want it to be flat. They don't want a flat life, flat dreams, flat hopes, a flat future... So what then?

You have to know that Brandon's head is entirely covered with rubber so no sound can escape from it. Just in case you wanted to hear anything from them.

They are swimming in this flatness, looking for curved elements.

Bradon can't see any curved elements. There are no waterfalls, nor holes through where the water could leave. The only thing they could see was an Octopus with bright eyes. They learned from him that the only way to get to the atmosphere was with one eye on water and one finger on wind. Without this code you can't follow the octopus.

A quintessential miracle.

The octopus opened Brandon's palm and placed a box in their hand.

"Here, take this. You might need it where you're going, to that place where kilograms have been redefined, where sexy ladies give birth to genderless babies and where water is but a simple liquid, once known to man."

Water knew where the genderless babies were, it tried to help but with no form or senses, how could it tell Brandon what they needed to know? They needed to be together in this. Nobody could know.

Teleportation was useful but selfish.

You could be in and out of time. Property, care, disasters, patriarchal structures all lost their dramaturgy. Brandon found themself in the palace garden.

The babies started talking to them.

"Knowledge is no longer knowledge. Words are no longer objects we collect in our memory. Objects are no longer physical beings we play with and destroy. Time has taken all of that away from us. Time has put it all in a small matchbox."

Brandon thought, I need a change I feel locked in. Where should I go now? I can't breathe, let me out of here. My whole body is craving for something that my mind is still not able to picture or frame. Am I doomed?'

I took out the glistering blob—the new healing matter invented by scientists—it is like a healing plasticine. While its forms may be different, it does not mean they are not all true. The plasticine can freeze and become solid or evaporate to gas.

The blob is then the solution Brandon thought and placed this glistering form into the sprinkler system. The choice seemed odd but they couldn't think of anything better to do. They hit the fire alarm, the sprinklers came on.

The water makes things reflective. Finally, an answer we could live with. Simply because it made us happy. That's all there was to know right?

Instead, here everything was possible. We started to design a new DNA chain that would substitute our old idea of a paradise. It's now here!

On earth this would be hard to realize, much less imagine.

There were of course attempts, as our brains have always been hardwired to see paradise. Green hills and a river is an aesthetic in our DNA. But back home nothing like this could be achieved.

Brandon thought to ask the babies to come with them to earth and enlighten everyone. They were afraid people might not accept.

Imprinted on their forehead they wore the code the Octopus had given them, proud like a jewel. When they arrived in the new world it would be a sign to recognize where they had come from.

They pulled it and it was connected to a small crystal-like rock. They were surprised the crystal was creating this sound.

michkin glock funze, abi szanla fe situ es. lalala ret mi contlaoa

Normally it is used to polarize sunlight and create a shadow even when our eyes cannot see.

It was a completely new starting point. The question was: How long would it take before the stars started to reflect our undesirable past upon us?

Sepake Angiama
Luz de Amor
Charlotte David
Pablo Esbert Lilienfeld
Thymios Fountas
Nada Gambia
Teresa Gentile
Rachel Himmelfarb
Byron Kalomamas
Laure Kervyn
Eszter Némethi
Kathi Seebeck
Federico Vladimir Strate Pezdirc
Maud Waregne
Fanny Zaman

The British newspaper the *Guardian* reported that following the UK polling day, the exit poll predicts an eighty-six-seat Tory landslide majority; the largest win since Maggie Thatcher. The news came as the last full moon emerged on the twelfth hour of the twelfth day of the twelfth month of the year, 2019.

Simultaneous to the conservatives win was the seemingly undetected infiltration of a female life form; one that only existed as a voice. No one noticed it at first as it seemingly took over all the vocal pre-recorded infrastructures of the island, such as those for transport announcements, apologizing for late trains, supermarket self-checkouts thanking customers for using their services etc. Even in telemarketing calls which were primarily meant to offer new mobile phone packages because of the shifting rates and tariffs, was the voice now heard. With the island now fully cut off from the mainland it meant that the voice needed to be brief, speaking only in short, abbreviated terms. Now. Less. Coverage. Now. Less. Contact.

My trip today might be the last one I am able to do with such ease to the mainland. I had been thinking a lot about Roman's bio-symbiotic neural cloud. I was testing a bit the chip he gave me and it was truly inspiring. So funny that we end up having more belief in the technology than the people, but then again, this cloud is for us. Not too many people have access to the bio-symbiotic neural cloud. It was the way in which we could share thoughts and feelings, love, loss and empathy without getting angry with people that often caused disputes, arguments, differing opinions and rioting. When we can no longer easily get to the mainland, some may find other ways to escape.

Roman's intelligence in this area was so advanced he could easily become a target. In the creation of Xandrompida, the voice for the millions of bits and bites of rotting code. The system could no longer sustain itself with the expense of emotional labor taxes being applied promised by the new government. The biosymbiotic cloud was leaking and the voice's entry into daily telecommunications was just the start. The fiber optic cables under the Channel were tenuous but Roman knew the only way to get to them was to understand a non-compliance in new terms, for the first time, a viable alternative. Him and the rest imagined something that was mutated but that could bring it down and relocate it to a different network—distributed amongst the ones that are willing to try it—I will bare it along my memories:

So they formed a party of non-compliance it was called New Terms, no longer would their voice be taken and represented by a disconnected trans, man or woman who did not care about the whole society but for just a small section. The cloud was still useful though, it had the capability of eliminating voices that induced fear. As they had recognized that fear could be incited in people by giving them plenty and then taking it away again. But this did not stop the New Terms who knew the power of language. Could they shift the algorithm in such a way that the bots could unlearn their fearful and gerrymandering vocabulary? Or did the whole apparatus need rebooting? There wasn't much more time to think. The results were in and the witch-hunt would begin soon for anyone who had voted for the others. The New Terms knew they had to reach out to more people. Essentially here is how it worked: you get a chip implanted, open source, which you can craft yourself. For the schematics you need connections. The implant connects to a sub-frequency of normal Wi-Fi, and then through the interface you can "save" experience, memories, ideas, etc. to someone else on the network and vice versa. What Roman envisioned was a decentralized cognition network that would use feminist organizational strategies, radical softness and hyper empathy in order to offset the continued capitalist system of desire that was born out of the '80s politics of Regan and Thatcher. They had created this desire for want, for surplus, for speculative desire for living. Xandrompida replaced Siri and infiltrated google searches that looked for keywords such as "stay" and "love." Simple and dangerous. Their mono-syllables could undo the complex cloud codification, scrambling hate speech into a series of inane emojis and fake news into cat memes. Xan—as the voice became known, was now in the heads of those who had opted in for the implants and navigation systems. But Roman didn't know if he could trust the New Terms. Was a party even the right term? He had to ask Xan if this could truly work. Roman is from a generation that has seen nothing work, financial crisis, division, hate; politics and mainstream opposition in this public stage meant failure. The only thing that was working was Xan, the chips, and the in-between, it is definitely hard to try to imagine when all revolution is historical and never present. Xan was also programmed not to understand capitalistic values. Social values always override anything that tried to create fiscal profit above the health of the social body and collective mind. The revolution was not televised but memorized. The brutality of that uprising, the pain and suffering was so vivid that it was felt by all. It began with Greta believing that people could force the change as the corporations continued to lie about reducing their emissions. But it was not her words that began the riots, an abrupt hiccup—a strike on the supplying coal mine trickled down to a massive shortage. Once the power went down the generators kicked in and in that split second the data was released. Closed conversations, dark tweets and supposedly deleted slack threads were unleashed into the world. And when the lights came back on, all hell had broken loose. Xan was the only force that could have contained the public rage—an outpouring of disillusion. But the cables couldn't take the heat. The northern villages felt it first, the warm soil, the static in the air.

The ones with the chip felt it; a weird moment of unsettling exposure, one moment where our network became visible, permeable.

Again, I get stopped at control, but this time they don't even know what I had taken with me.

I was bringing the Rock of Afes, which is a place where we call all to gather when we are low on hope and belief for a better world. It's a moment of connection between human and non-human species and all life forms. We come to it, in a moment where life can no longer be transformed, we come to it when all communication fails.

There would at least be one good thing that could come out of this gathering that left a scar on our bodies, we saw how it actually is, to live just for the self. The network manifested for all that were part of it a decentralized self. Contradicting our recently lost, collective repository, it made visible the life of self-destruction, the circle of life contorted and broken.

We meet here because this is the place where it all began. Before we uploaded the dreams of community.

It's beginning to rain and the smell of scorched circuits is still in the air. Let their minerals return to the earth. Every design must have a death cycle, a way to say farewell.[1] And here at the Rock, is where the end begins.

Sepake Angiama
Clare Butcher
Byron Kalomamas

1 With thanks to Suzanne Kite for her continuing work around Lakota epistemologies in AI and learning machine design processes, shared during her workshop *Future, Fire, Fiction: storytelling workshop for imagining future technologies through design justice and Indigenous philosophy*, co-led with Una Lee, October 24, 2019, Toronto Biennial of Art.

Quenton Miller

Afterword: Drama!

If Nature has so wove her web of kindness that some threads of love and desire are entangled with the piece—must the whole web be rent in drawing them out?

—Lawrence Sterne[1]

1 Lawrence Sterne, *A Sentimental Journey Through France and Italy* (1768)

"Plotting" often means giving tension to a tale by arranging events, after the fact. In a secondary definition, "plotting" characters make monstrous or at least sinister-vibed schemes in advance of the action. Together plots are themes "warped with various situational motifs... placed in tension like yarns on a loom before the weaving begins."[2]

Like in a love triangle, plots make shapes and structure relations. Yet because they get their momentum from lack (of money, love, evidence, et cetera), this does not end well. This DNA of doom travels through time, from place to place, where "labyrinths of linkages reemerge in the same old place, after the disintegration of old ways of life."[3] *Plots are spells, with actualizing effects, and must be handled with care—or else!*

What follows are some cautionary tales, about stories and life plotting against each other...

2 Literary critic Viktor Shklovsky, who worked in the framework of Russian formalist criticism: A loose group of literary critics including Vladimir Propp and Mikhail Bakhtin, looking for rules and schema in the structure of stories. Often in pleasingly abstract ways: "In art, blood is not bloody. No, it just rhymes with 'flood'" said Shklovsky, who was born in the late 1800s, and died in a Moscow hospital in 1984. Viktor Shklovsky, *Bowstring: On the Dissimilarity of the Similar*, trans. Shushan Avagyan (Champaign: Dalkey Archive Press, [1970] 2011).

3 Viktor Shklovsky, *Energy of Delusion: A Book on Plot*, trans. Shushan Avagyan (1981). Shklovsky wrote in Russian, using the terms *syuzhet* and *fabula*—similar to "plot" and "story" in English.

The first begins at Berkeley University, a sunny campus the size of a town, with perfect, melon-green grass. But something is wrong. One graduate student claimed to have gotten rid of a professor's advances only after setting her dog after him one night. A later article in the New Republic confirmed that among the student body this professor "had a reputation as a 'seducer' of graduate students at best—and a predator at worst."[4]

Franco Moretti, meanwhile, is a famous academic whose methods imported a mass of new books into academic research. Books he delighted in never having read: that's what computers were for! Moretti was the key figure in the "digital humanities" (a term for using software to study books in mass), reviewing thousands of books in one go (*Style Inc.: Reflections on 7,000 Titles*) and diagramming story structures in neutral graphs and lines (*Graphs, Maps, Trees: Abstract Models for a Literary History*).

Elif Batuman, a student of Moretti, described the situation: "instead of theology we need 'a little pact with the devil'; we surrender the reading of individual texts, and in return we will get: 'concepts.'"[5] The price, for this ghoulish ability to read more than could ever fit down living eyeballs, was to flatten stories into machine-readable plots.[6] The Stanford Literary Lab was set up for this new networked literature. At the center of the web, like a spider, was Franco Moretti.[7]

4 Irene Hsu and Rachel Stone, "A Professor Is Kind of Like a Priest," *The New Republic* (November 30, 2017), newrepublic.com/article/146049/a-professor-kind-like-priest

5 Elif Batuman, *Adventures of a Man of Science, N+1* (2005) https://nplusonemag.com/issue-3/reviews/adventures-of-a-man-of-science/

6 A vision of literature that "will become 'second hand': a patchwork of other people's research, without a single direct textual reading" Franco Moretti, *Distant Reading* (London: Verso, 2013).

7 A side track from the main thread: The distinction between Moretti's work and the Russian formalist critics quoted here is outlined by Jessica Merrill: "The study of traveling plots goes back at least to the influential work of the German philologist Theodore Benfey, who sought to trace a common stock of tales found in Europe to their Indian origins, developing what became known in folklore studies as the 'theory of borrowing'… A premise Moretti shares with these Russian (formalist) theorists is that to study the history of plots, one must posit that literary narrative can be thought of as being stratified. Moretti, with his gift for simplification, puts it as follows:

Then comes the defendant: Kimberly Latta, who attended UC Berkley as a graduate student in Comparative Literature in 1985. "Franco demonstrated a great deal of interest in me, and I foolishly believed it was because he found me intelligent," Latta wrote about how Moretti spoke a world into being where "professors in Italy routinely slept with their graduate students." Simultaneously, Latta's coming of age story became "jumpy, disjointed, incoherent" and shaken out of sequence. After a status upgrade on campus, being invited to staff parties, he was "pushing me down onto my futon... "No." I remember I said... "I don't want to."

"Don't tell me his name" the university official in charge of reporting sexual violence later said. "I had already told her enough about an Italian visiting professor, in the English department, for her to know who he was."[8]

Moretti denied that he raped Latta, saying they had "fully consensual sex" and he was "horrified by the accusation." Latta additionally claimed that "When I told Franco Moretti I had told Frances Ferguson (the university official) that he was sexually harassing me, he said that if I pressed charges he would ruin my career," which Moretti also denies.

This will go into an odd concoction of plots and magic, where non-meaningful patterns and fictional or abstract entities might, in the end, exercise as much power as direct causation. My own plot of the events is hinged on a hex: Moretti told Latta she was "beautiful like Mathilde in The Red and the Black."[9]

'foreign plot; local characters'... As the stratum of the text that persists over time formally and moves geographically, it would seem that plot is a key unit of analysis for the study of world literature. But how are we to approach it in quantitative terms? Moretti's last chapter in *Distant Reading*, 'Network Theory, Plot Analysis' proposes that plot can be quantified using network theory... This is a departure from the Russian tradition, which approaches plot in terms of the actions of the dramatis personae." Jessica Merrill, "Distant Reading in Russia: Franco Moretti and the Formalist Tradition," *Eurozine* (2 May, 2018), https://www.eurozine.com/distant-reading-russia-franco-moretti-formalist-tradition/

8 Kimberly Latta, *What Happened at Berkeley* (2017) https://www.academia.edu/35221195/What_Happened_at_Berkeley_docx

9 Ibid.

"STENDHAL SYNDROME"

Mathilde de la Mole is a character from Stendhal's novel *The Red and the Black* (1830), a fictional anti-heroine with a mindful of freakish kinks and dreams.

In *The Red and the Black*, the central character is Julien Sorel. If relations in the novel are mapped over characters on campus, then Moretti must equal the hero Julien. Julien is the handsome son of a carpenter who plots his way up in the world by seducing society ladies. After landing a job tutoring the local Mayor's kids, he elopes with the deeply religious mother of the family, Madame de Rênal.

Through social connections he goes on to work for powerful Marquis de la Mole. Sorel forcefully and opportunistically elopes with the Marquis' daughter Mathilde, the richest spinster in town (more on that later, note here Latta's dramatic personae enters the story). Their marriage is about to go ahead when a letter from Madame de Rênal arrives, addressed to Mathilde's father the Marquis. It calls Julien Sorel opportunistic, calls for his cancellation, and between the lines calls Julien back to his old lover. He does return, only with a mind full of violence.

DELICIOUS VACCINES

An exhaustively trodden theme comes to the surface: to engage critically with a drama of passions brings the critic seductively close to it, becoming vulnerable to reproducing the plot all over again. The plot is nonhuman, a devil. It presents a different yet already-existing reality as it seeks contagion from its world to yours.

In *The Red and the Black*, Stendhal attributes this threat of novels—which not only relay bad behavior, but step into the very shoes of bad people—to his worse characters: "Once in the house, these dangerous books would corrupt Madame's servants." This could be a parody of Plato banishing poetry in his ideal society: an old plot (do representations of bad actions cause bad actions?) that resonates through time.[10] Plots can inoculate, but how much vaccine turns into the disease itself?

10 "Ah, Sir, a novel is a mirror carried along a high road. At one moment it reflects to your vision the azure skies, at another the mire of the puddles at your feet. And the man who carries this mirror in his pack will be accused by you of being immoral! His mirror shews the mire, and you blame the mirror! Rather blame that high road upon which the puddle lies, still more the inspector of roads who allows the water to gather and the puddle to form." Stendhal, *Le Rouge et le Noir* (1830), quoted by Hans Ulrich Gumbrecht in "The Roads of the Novel," in *The Novel, Volume 2: Forms and Themes*, ed. Franco Moretti (New Jersey: Princeton University Press, 2006).

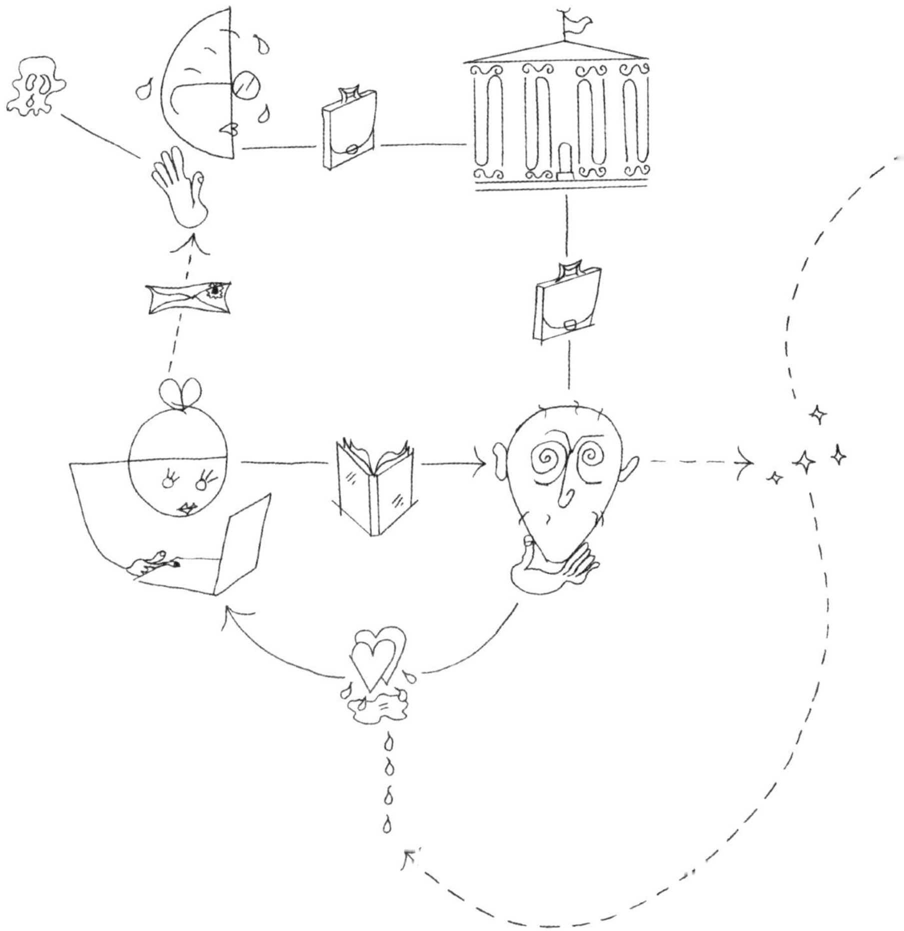

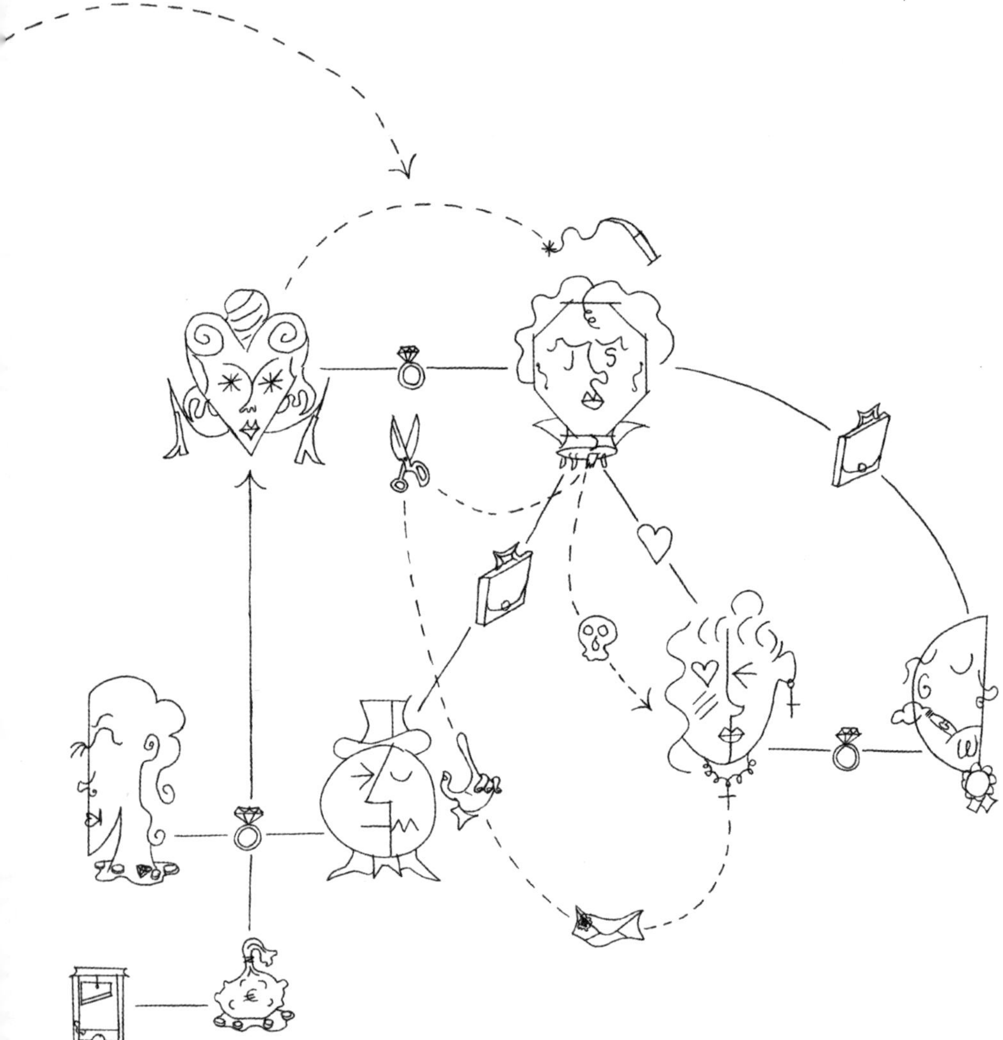

ENEMY AIRTIME

BY NOMINATING LATTA  AS MATHILDE , DID IT SET A WORLD-MAKING STRUCTURE IN MOTION? DID ALL THESE PLOTS MORETTI WAS NOMINATING REALLY HAVE FUTURES HIBERNATING INSIDE OF THEM? WAS MORETTI  BECOMING JULIAN SOREL , HIGH ON PLOTS FROM ALL THOSE YEARS OF HUFFING HISTORICAL VIOLENCE? AND ONCE A PLOT STRUCTURE IS APPLIED, MUST IT BE KEPT TO THE BITTER END?

GENRE MAGIC

Plots in their abstract shapes do not exist in our world, they're a sum of reappearances. The corners of a love triangle must be somewhere (and somewhere again) in a configuration of time, place and genre called a "chronotope" by another structuralist literary critic, Mikhail Bakhtin. The instability in occupying a plot doesn't just apply to the live situation. In turn the chronotope transforms the plot's generic shape. The connection between plots and situations, between names and concrete particulars, is magic. The active ingredient to make magic work is belief.

Anthropologist and folklorist James Frazer split his theory of magic into two strands. Imitational magic operates via metaphors and similarity. Here what comes upon the imitation comes upon the original. The second strand is contagion: magic taking effect through physical contact, lingering even after the touch stops. In the space of plotting, two dimensions of causality warp each other: instead of. In concrete situations, abstract plots emerge with their imitational magic. In myths, the living sites of the story warp the plot with concrete particulars.

Under the slippery spell of plot, a tenuous connection like a speech or thought bubble can be just as touching as other social fictions: say, a marriage or employment contract. Every node in this network is an agent, every node a feasible protagonist,[11] and can think for themselves and not the author: Napoleon, the moon, a gun, a guillotine.

11 Take, for example, the Chinese story of someone dreaming a butterfly, who awakes unsure of whether they dreamed the butterfly or the butterfly dreamed them.

A plot is a structure whose shape anticipates relations. It can potentially be infinite, but when you open your mouth it extends only as far as a communicable field of causality. The shape traces sense across a web of pre-existing drives: The crafty character, the scheming state imagination, the sponsor's stratagem, the institution's intrigue, the director's designs. They are frameworks, not fixed futures.

The plotting of story structures over life achieves maximum magic in Etienne Souriau's 1950 book, *The Two Hundred Thousand Dramatic Situations*, a tarot-like system for plots: as in *all* plots. Souriau calculates exactly 210,141 structures by exhausting possible dramatic relations featuring six elements: the lion (or strength) ♌, the sun (desired by the lion) ☉, the receiving star (the earth, farmer of the sun) ♁, Mars (the opponent) ♂, Libra (the arbiter of the situation) ♎, and the moon (the mirror of force and helping agent) ☾. The elements being pulled from the tarot deck—alternate to Moretti's lab coated language—suggests divination, yet as well as an actualizing prediction, tarot can be a consciously interpretive exercise to re-protagonize where you sit in the web.

Unlike the straight lines of network theory, plotting introduces dramatic tension and texture, which means it's not strictly a topology. One of the Victor Shklovsky books I'm quoting from is named *Bowstring* after a Heraclitus quote, on how conflicting textures make music. Later in Shklovsky's book the musical bowstring has stretched into the type that shoots: a plot is pulled tight and "the arrow of intensified emotion is released." A plot, in its different areas and angles can be saggy or highly strung. Moretti, quoting a colleague in a *New York Times* article, defined a protagonist as "the character that minimized the sum of the distances to all other vertices."[12] But from the perspective of drama it's not the number of links giving an actor its power, but the tension wired up in it. Links are an action, they can bend, force, exercise unequal weighting and privilege. What is a snake in one direction can be a ladder in the other. A thought bubble can be a tractor beam that physically connect you to what it circles. Physics, facts, footwear, faeries, and the personal response twine into the relational canopy. The dramatic-semantic overview is like a poorly constructed geodesic dome on the verge of collapsing or snapping into a new equilibrium. The invisible kinetic force keeps us rapt: Who knows when it will pop? (Least of all the dome.)

Links can be soft, stiff, dry, amorous, bristling, flexible, imprisoning, gendered, dripping, overbearing, ticklish or a fatal noose. To escape the hex of Moretti, the links and nodes of plot could, taking Eve Kosofsky Sedgwick's definition of queer, "refuse to signify monolithically."[13] Sedgwick takes the word queer to mean *across*—reminiscing on the German word *quer* (transverse) or Latin *torquere* (to twist), as in "plot twist": that point of re-signification where things, as everyone knows, are not what they seem.

12 Quoted in Kathryn Schulz, "The Mechanic Muse: What Is Distant Reading?" *The New York Times* (June 24, 2011).

13 Eve Kosofsky Sedgwick, *Tendencies* (Durham: Duke University Press, 1993).

INTERMEZZO: MIDNIGHT ACCOUNTING

A fable: An owl, holding an audio recorder between its beak, is interviewing a possum for a newspaper: *The Nightly Hoot*. It's 2011, maybe 2012, during the financial crisis. "The Greeks gave us logic," says the possum. "We owe them for that. It was Aristotle who came up with the big 'therefore.' We use this word millions of times, to make our most important decisions. It's about time we started paying for it. If every time we used the word therefore, we paid ten euros to Greece, the Greek financial crisis would be over in one day." The owl's beak drops down in surprise and the recorder falls to the ground, but the possum continues. "We have the technology to track down all those therefores. Every time Angela Merkel tells the Greeks we lent you all this money, therefore you must pay us back with interest, she must therefore first pay them their royalties." [14]

14 Fiachra Gibbons, "Film is over. What to do?," *The Guardian* (July 12, 2011), https://www.theguardian.com/film/2011/jul/12/jean-luc-godard-film-socialisme (I changed the characters.)

FICTION AS GROOMING

Plots can be a vaccine against themselves: "Plots use the contradictions of epochs," Viktor Shklyovsky said. "The adventures Shakespeare adopts from the Italian novella[15] (*Romeo and Juliet, Othello*...) are weakened, they show a different kind of reality." In *Hamlet*: the specific pickle of Orestes, a set of structural relations, is reused from the eponymous Greek tragedy: "the son of a murdered father, has to take vengeance on the murderer's wife—but the murderer's wife is his own mother... Hamlet is not only the descendent of Orestes... he is also someone who ponders his act, a reflective generation that evaluates the past." The plot returns with a new costume, like *Romeo and Juliet or Othello*, taken from Italian tales and replayed as tragedies, like the all-female version of *Ghostbusters*. From generation to generation, the young choose a style of looking back at the past, imitating it, and the distance between drafts is a whole direction of movement. "Plots use the contradictions of epochs, they insert in them new contradictions but maintain the old structures. We live simultaneously in multiple temporal realms."

15 Stendhal, like Shakespeare, borrowed plot structures extensively from violent, sexed-up Italian tales, even recording and rewriting his own collection, published in English under the title *Italian Chronicles* (Minnesota: Minnesota Press, 2017).

INTERMEZZO: A THEFT

A tourist strolls exotic destinations with her wallet drooping out her pocket. To no one's astonishment it's stolen. The tourist, who also happens to be a magician, follows the pickpockets,[16] hoping to outfox them by stealing her own wallet back. Someone films with a covert camera. The pickpockets are unionized and have their guard down in this respect. On her toes, the tourist-slash-magician disappears into a cloud of other tourists, and returns—with her own wallet! Now, full disclosure, the tourist who is also a magician is also a documentary filmmaker. Now, how to approach the pickpocket now and not appear as a sneaky cop? She requests an on-camera interview. They exchange some tips and tricks: the joy of technique and speed and rhythm! But at a point a cloud appears over the pickpocket. She is ashamed of what she does. Why apologize to a magician!? The ethical queasiness comes in a rush, what's being pickpocketed is not a wallet inasmuch as a soul sucked through the air on-camera. The pickpocket's mood does not last and the pickpocket becomes friendly again, maybe with a speed that's a little menacing. They invite the tourist-magician documentary filmmaker further into the forest for a drink. She goes, she is surrounded on all sides at tight quarters by the union of pickpockets, you could even say "escorted" but lacking nothing in confidence she is joyously carried by the crowd, like a puppy following smells into the spring.

16 Pickpockets work with a decoy and third bystander to carry the wallet off.

The act of nominating Latta as Mathilde transposed a sinister and all too authoritative system over campus life, demarcating active and passive elements, managing flows and modes of desiring.

The method of fixing narratives in profane gists, approaching the material as an un-implicated scientist with a blind eye to its speculative-incantive nature, was maybe itself a fiction, akin to the awakening-the-mummy moment in a horror movie. It's hard to imagine racy dramas *not* being inflected with teacher-student relations.[17]

Returning to *The Red and the Black*: we should talk about Julien's actions toward Mathilde in the book. Julien (Moretti) plots to make Mathilde (Latta) fall for him by forging love letters addressed to himself, letters that plot himself as a legitimate object of desire for a comparable (high-society/younger) girl.

And Mathilde is a proto-goth with a kink for violence and a loose relation to consent. At one point she is "thrilled to the bottom of her soul... (and) could think of nothing but the happiness of having almost been killed" (by Julien Sorel). Prosper Mérimée said that Stendhal "always seemed convinced by the idea, much canvassed under the Empire, that any woman may be taken by storm and that it is up to every man to attempt it."

In Latta's account of the alleged rape by Moretti, he told her "You American girls, you always say no when you mean yes."[18] But we could say: "You nineteenth century French fictional characters, you always say no when you mean yes." "I remember being paralyzed and terrified," recalled Latta.[19]

17 The question of which texts were on Moretti's curriculum is open to speculation.

18 Kimberly Latta, *What Happened at Berkeley* (2017), https://www.academia.edu/35221195/What_Happened_at_Berkeley_docx

19 Emily Deruy, "In university sexual harassment cases, a chilling power dynamic," *East Bay Times* (December 7, 2017) https://www.eastbaytimes.com/2017/12/07/in-university-sexual-harassment-cases-a-chilling-power-dynamic/

PLOT TWIST

Latta later described a chance meeting on an airplane where Moretti approached in the guise of a fond old friend. If early on she was young and guileless, now she was not without agency. Latta recalled the sheer mental presence required to summon a different storyline and how, when she did, Moretti "turned away, ran back [down the plane aisle]"[20] —plot in flames.

20 Kimberly Latta, *What Happened at Berkeley* (2017), https://www.academia.edu/35221195/What_Happened_at_Berkeley_docx

SILK PRISONS

Stendhal called writing a "silk prison," which could refer to being trapped in the weave as well as the texture of the overall canopy. To some extent the trap is inherent in the force of drama itself, a tensioning and knotting of powers, usually propelled through time by lack. "The narrative of happiness" says literary critic D. A. Miller,[21] "is inevitably frustrated by the fact that only insufficiencies, defaults, deferrals, can be 'told.'" It's fitting that Shakespeare and Stendhal, when they wrote about "love and desire,"[22] looked back to folk tales for the ready-made stock archetypes of "revenge, bloody daggers, poisonings, and thick-walled nunneries."[23] Often in their most mythy, plot summaries repeat trajectories based on lack, yet these sets of relations, like a spread of tarot cards, shouldn't be considered as eternally fixed archetypes, it's the topology of relations that tells you who you are. Once that's given, plot structures can twist, agents can be repositioned and re-protagonized. In the geometry of vicious cycles, new forms of relation must spring.

21 D. A. Miller, *Narrative and its Discontents* (Princeton New Jersey: Princeton University Press, 1989).

22 The epigraph, again.

23 The blurb from Stendhal's *Italian Chronicles*, collected in English in 1999.

INTO AND OUT OF LAW

"In order to talk in court, you need to talk well; those who weren't good orators engaged people to write appeals, which were very much like books… a man complaining about his wife's infidelity says that his house has creaky stairs. This is one of the first realistic details of a psychological novel ever written down."[24]

THE MORETTI-LATTA CASE DID NOT GO TO COURT.[25] LATTA'S ACCOUNT REMAINS ON HER ACADEMIA.EDU PAGE. INSTEAD OF GOING INTO LEGAL STORYTELLING, MORETTI SLIPPED AWAY INTO THE WORLD OF LITERATURE.

24 Viktor Shklovsky, *On the Theory of Prose*, trans. Alexandra Berlina (1983).

25 Where individual assault is difficult to make-fact in the realm of law, migrating plots, as in a pattern repeated by a perpetrator across testimonies, can produce a public "proof" on social platforms.

Sepake Angiama is the artistic director of the Institute for International Visual Art (iniva) in London. The institution hosts the Stuart Hall Library and is dedicated to supporting the praxis of thinking through and working with the complexity of the effect of globalization and hybridization of culture on social and political ontologies, epistemologies and pedagogies. Angiama's praxis stems from radical pedagogies, black feminist thought, rethinking human/ non-human relation, and roots itself in how we might imagine and inhabit the world *otherwise*.

Lietje Bauwens studied philosophy in Amsterdam and works as a writer and editor for multiple cultural magazines and platforms. Under the name 431, she and Wouter De Raeve initiate artistic research frameworks such as *Perhaps it is high time for a xeno-architecture to match* (Sternberg Press, 2018), *the new local* (2018) and most recently the film project *WTC A Love Story* (2020). She was an artist in residence at the Jan van Eyck Academy 2018–19 and is an editor for *nY Magazine*.

Kate Briggs is a writer and translator based in Rotterdam, NL. She is the author of *This Little Art* (Fitzcarraldo Editions, 2017), an essay on the practice of literary and philosophical translation, based in part on the experience of translating Roland Barthes' *How to Live Together* and *The Preparation of the Novel* (Columbia University Press, 2013 and 2011). She is working on a new book, titled *The Long Form*, on care, attention, duration and the novel. She teaches at the Piet Zwart Institute, Rotterdam.

Federico Campagna is a philosopher and the author of *Prophetic Culture: recreation for adolescents* (2021), *Technic and Magic: The Reconstruction of Reality* (2018), *The Last Night: anti-Work, Atheism, Adventure* (2013), and *What We Are Fighting For: a Radical Collective Manifesto* (2012).

Alex Carp is a research editor at the *New York Times Magazine*. He also co-chairs the Brooklyn Book Festival's nonfiction committee, and is a contributor to the *New York Magazine*. For four years, he was an editor for the *Voice of Witness* book series, and previously an editor at *Guernica*.

The work of Mette Edvardsen is situated within the performing arts field as a choreographer and performer. Although some of her works explore other media or formats, such as video, books and writing, her interest is always in their relationship to the performing arts as a practice and a situation. She has worked for several years as a dancer and performer for a number of companies and projects, and has developed her own work since 2002. She presents her works internationally and continues to develop projects with other artists, both as a collaborator and as a performer. A retrospective of her work was presented at Black Box theatre in Oslo in 2015, and the focus program *Idiorritmias* at MACBA in Barcelona in 2018. Her project *Time has fallen asleep in the afternoon sunshine* is ongoing since 2010, and has its base now at the headquarters of osloBiennalen first edition 2019–2024 in Oslo. She is currently a research fellow at Oslo National Academy of the Arts.

Jamie Fisher is a research editor at the *New York Times Magazine*. She writes criticism for the *London Review of Books*, the *L.A. Review of Books*, *BOMB*, the *Times Literary Supplement, and The Millions*. Her fiction has appeared in *n+1*, *Subtropics*, and the *Literary Review*. She is working on a collection of short stories and a novel.

Tristan Garcia is professor of Philosophy at the University of Lyon and an award-winning novelist. He is the author of *La vie intense: Une obsession modern* (Autrement, 2016), translated into English as *The Life Intense: A Modern Obsession* (Edinburgh University

Press, 2018) and *Forme et objet. Un traité des choses* (Presses Universitaires de France, 2011), translated into English as *Form and Object: A Treatise on Things* (Edinburgh University Press, 2014). His other philosophical works include *L'Image and Nous* (Arlea, 2010). His fictional works include *Les cordelettes de Browser, En l'absence de classement final and Mémoires de la jungle*. In 2008, he received the Prix de Flore for *La meilleure part des hommes* (Editions Gallimard, 2010), translated into English as *Hate: A Romance* (Farrar, Straus and Giroux, 2010).

Maryam Monalisa Gharavi is an artist, poet, and theorist whose work explores the interplay between aesthetic and political valences in the public domain. Her work in film, video, text, performance, drawing, and internetal form has appeared in various global exhibitions. Book publications include a translation of Waly Salomão's *Algaravias: Echo Chamber* (Ugly Duckling Presse), nominated for a PEN Award for Poetry in Translation; *The Distancing Effect* (BlazeVOX); and *Bio* (Inventory Press). Artist books/chapbooks include *Apparent Horizon 2* (Bonington Gallery); *Alphabet of an Unknown City* (Belladonna*), *Secret Catalan Poem* (The Elephants), *Mohammad Wikipedia Book* (Recess), and *Dictionary of Night*, co-authored with Mirene Arsanios (Ashkal Alwan). She completed a Ph.D. at Harvard University and an M.F.A. at Bard College. She lives and works in New York.

Nicoline van Harskamp is an Amsterdam-based artist whose work considers acts of language and communication in relation to ideology and solidarity through video, installation, and scripted performance. Her live pieces were staged, among other places, at Steirischer Herbst in Graz, Tate Modern in London, KunstWerke in Berlin, Witte de With in Rotterdam, New Museum in New York, Stedelijk Museum Bureau in Amsterdam; Arnolfini in Bristol; Serralves Foundation in Porto; and the Kaaitheater in Brussels. She is a Professor for Performative Art at the University of Fine Arts in Münster, Germany. See also: www.vanharskamp.net and www.englishes-mooc.org

Quenton Miller is an artist and writer whose bodies of work include *The Trial* (Stedelijk Museum Bureau Amsterdam, 2016) about the ICC in the Hague, the support group *Dying Marxists* (Athens Biennale, 2018) which continues through discursive events and memorials, and the *Interior* (with the archive of Office for Metropolitan Architecture, 2021). He works across fiction, format and modes of address in films, drawings, sculptures, publications and plays, working in collaboration with narrative subjects like professional pickpockets and Tito's parrot Koki. He is co-founder of the artist-run space When Site Lost the Plot in Amsterdam and was a resident at the Jan van Eyck Academy 2018–19.

Ingo Niermann is a writer and the editor of the speculative "Solution Series" at Sternberg Press. Recent books include *Solution 295–304: Mare Amoris* (2020), *Burial of the White Man* (with Erik Niedling, 2019), *It's Me!* (with David Pearce, 2019), and *Solution 275–294: Communists Anonymous* (ed., with Joshua Simon, 2017). Based on his novel *Solution 257: Complete Love* (2016), Niermann initiated the *Army of Love*, a project that tests and promotes a just redistribution of sensual love. www.ingoniermann.com

Michael Portnoy is a New York-based multimedia artist. Coming from a background in dance and experimental comedy, his performance-based work employs a variety of media: from film and participatory installations to theater, sculpture, writing, painting, and curation. He has presented internationally in museums, art galleries and theaters, including recently Steirischer Herbst, Graz, Austria (2019 & 2018); Akademie der Künste der Welte, Cologne, Germany (2017); KW Institute for Contemporary Art, Berlin, Germany (2017); Playground, STUK, Leuven, Belgium (2016, 2014); Liverpool Biennial, Liverpool, UK (2016); Witte de With, Rotterdam, The Netherlands (2016); the Centre Pompidou, Paris, France (2015); Stedelijk Museum, Amsterdam, The Netherlands (2014); Palais de Tokyo, Paris,

France (2013); The Kitchen, New York, USA (2013); dOCUMENTA 13, Kassel, Germany (2012); 11th Baltic Triennial (co-curator), Vilnius, Lithuania (2012); and the Taipei Biennial, Taipei, Taiwan (2010). He is a visiting professor at Malmö Art Academy. For more information visit: strangergames.com

Achal Prabhala is a writer and researcher in Bangalore, India. He runs the AccessIBSA project, which campaigns for access to medicines in India, Brazil & South Africa. He writes in small literary magazines around the world, including *Chimurenga*, *Transition*, *Bidoun* & *Africa Is a Country*. Currently, he is working on expanding access to treatments and vaccines in the coronavirus pandemic, and on a novel.

Karoline Świeżyński (1982, Wadern, Germany) is a graphic designer based in Amsterdam, whose work has experimented with text, countercultural aesthetics, and fiction in design. She joins ventures with artists and culturally involved initiatives, working with academic and non-academic writers, photographers, and performers. Her paper-based and digital publications are sensitive to site-specific context, uncovering formal and non-formal links. Świeżyński graduated in 2011 from the Gerrit Rietveld Academy in Amsterdam. In 2018–19 she participated in the post-graduate program at the Jan van Eyck Academy in Maastricht. www.looklooklook.org

Wolfgang Tillmans (born 1968, Remscheid, Germany) is an artist who lives and works in Berlin and London. Since the early 1990s he has created work that has epitomized a new kind of subjectivity in photography, pairing intimacy and playfulness with social critique and the persistent questioning of existing values and hierarchies. Through his seamless integration of genres, subjects, techniques, and exhibition strategies, he has expanded conventional ways of approaching the medium, and his practice continues to address the fundamental question of what it means to create pictures in an increasingly image-saturated world.

Robert Trafford is a journalist and researcher with Forensic Architecture, specializing in "open source" investigative research. Forensic Architecture (FA) is a research agency based at Goldsmiths, University of London. The agency undertakes advanced spatial and media investigations into cases of human rights violations, with and on behalf of communities affected by political violence, human rights organizations, international prosecutors, environmental justice groups, and media.

COLOPHON

Speculative Facts
Onomatopee 177

Publisher Onomatopee

Editorial concept Lietje Bauwens, Quenton Miller, Karoline Świeżyński

Introduction Lietje Bauwens and Quenton Miller
Commissioned texts Sepake Angiama, Alex Carp & Jamie Fisher (*New York Times Magazine*), Tristan Garcia, Maryam Monalisa Gharavi, Ingo Niermann, Achal Prabhala, Robert Trafford (Forensic Architecture)
Interviews Achal Prabhala (with Africa Check, WikiAfrica, *Fact Factories & Chimurenga*), Lietje Bauwens (with Tristan Garcia)
Workshops Kate Briggs, Mette Edvardsen, Nicoline van Harskamp, Michael Portnoy
Image and text Wolfgang Tillmans
Diagrams Federico Campagna
Afterword Quenton Miller

Editorial Lietje Bauwens and Quenton Miller in conversation with Karoline Świeżyński

Graphic design Karoline Świeżyński in conversation with Quenton Miller

Copy editing Liz Allen

Print Printon AS, Tallinn, EST
Lithography High Trade, NL
Paper Munken Print White 1.5 90g/m², Serixo 80g/m² & 190g/m²
Edition 1400

Typefaces Difficult Times by Ronja Andersen, Times, Arial, Helvetica Rounded, Baskerville

Note on the type Elements of the typeface Times have been rearranged, mirrored, and rotated creating a new cut called Difficult Times. All letters are on first viewing still legible and recognizable, but on a closer look they appear off. Difficult Times can be seen as an additional cut to the Times family making it possible not only to set a text in regular, italics, or bold, but also in difficult. —Ronja Andersen

Special thanks to Huib Haye van der Werf, Solange Roosen, Lyndon Barrois Jr., Yasmine Ostendorf, Caszimir Cleutjens, Isabelle Sully, Ilke Gers, Hera Chan, Ronja Andersen, Jorrit Smit, Freek Lomme, Joannette van der Veer, Perri Mackenzie, Léa Lagasse, Lisa Miller

Thanks to the participants Lyndon Barrois Jr, Marissa Lee Benedict, Annabelle Binnerts, Andrea Canepa, Addoley Dzegede, Rob Hamelijnck, Julius Heinemann, Anna Ihle, Hasabie Kidanu, Christopher Meerdo, Daniel de Paula, Kristina Sedlerova-Villanen, Giulio Squillacciotti, Elisa Strinna, Nienke Terpsma, Maria Gil Ulldemolins, Katja Verheul, Ben Weir, Rain Wu

Kindly supported by Creative Industries Fund NL, Jan van Eyck Academy

creative industries fund NL   jan van eyck academie